The Cuban Hustle

The Cuban Hustle

CULTURE,
POLITICS,
EVERYDAY
LIFE

Sujatha Fernandes

Duke University Press Durham and London 2020

Designed by Drew Sisk
Typeset in Portrait Text and Canela Text
by Copperline Book Services

Library of Congress Cataloging-in-Publication Data Names:
Fernandes, Sujatha, author.
Title: The Cuban hustle : culture, politics, everyday life /
Sujatha Fernandes.
Description: Durham : Duke University Press, 2020.
Identifiers: LCCN 2019054785 (print) |
LCCN 2019054786 (ebook) |
ISBN 9781478008705 (hardcover) |
ISBN 9781478009641 (paperback) |
ISBN 9781478012269 (ebook)
Subjects: LCSH: Arts—Political aspects—Cuba. | Arts, Cuban
—20th century. | Arts and society—Cuba. | Socialism and
the arts—Cuba—History—20th century. | Cuba—
Intellectual life—20th century. | Cuba—
Cultural policy.
Classification: LCC NX180.P64 F48 2020 (print) |
LCC NX180.P64 (ebook) | DDC 700.97291/0904—dc23
LC record available at https://lccn.loc.gov/2019054785
LC ebook record available at https://lccn.loc.gov/2019054786

Cover art: The annual rap festival in Alamar, on the eastern
outskirts of Havana, Cuba. Photo by Adam Eastland.

For Norma Guillard

ACKNOWLEDGMENTS

I thank my colleagues, family, friends, and editors, who offered invaluable help and support in writing and compiling these essays. Norma Guillard has been part of this journey from my first trip to Cuba in 1998, and I dedicate this book to her, an inspiring and tireless warrior and a dear friend and confidante. Alex Halkin helped facilitate many connections and story ideas, and I am ever grateful for her and for the work of her extraordinary organization, Americas Media Initiative. Roane Carey at *The Nation* is a brilliant editor whose light touch and deep appreciation for the nuances of Cuba helped shape the essays. My editor at Duke, Miriam Angress, offered much enthusiasm and expert guidance, helping bring the essay collection to its final form. Two anonymous reviewers provided valuable feedback.

My heartfelt thanks go also to Agustín Drake, Leonor Jorge-Vergara, Lilia Cruz Marin, Randy Acosta, Hilda and Carlos Torres, Tonel, Elio Rodríguez, Alejandro Velasco, Kandice Chuh, Julie Skurski, Laura Weiss, Jacquelyn Kovarik, Michelle Chase, Milena Recio, Papito, Pipo and the Los Chapuserios community, Juan Carlos Baños Fernández, Roberto Zurbano, Magia López Cabrera, Alexey Rodríguez, Pablo Herrera, Julio Cardenas, Ariel Fernández, Tania Bruguera, Honor Jones, Gisela Arandia, Alejandro de la Fuente, Catherine Murphy, and Jason Stanyek.

I owe a big thanks to Matt Rogers, Alex Halkin, and Alejandro Ramírez Anderson for permission to use their photos in the book.

The members of my family, as always, have provided crucial support and encouragement: my husband, Mike; our children, Aisha and Shaad; my parents, Joe and Sylvie; and my sister, Deepa.

Material from "Public Art and Art Collectives in Havana," "New Cuban Cinema: Race and Sexuality," and "Cultural *Cimarronaje*: Afro-Cuban Visual Arts" is drawn in part from my book *Cuba Represent! Cuban Arts, State Power, and the Making of New Revolutionary Cultures* (Duke University Press, 2006). Material from "The Capital of Rap: Hip Hop Culture in Alamar" is drawn in part from my book *Close to the Edge: In Search of the Global Hip Hop Generation* (Verso, 2011).

INTRODUCTION

When the Soviet Union began its precipitous collapse in the late 1980s, the severe upheaval experienced by Cuban society, so heavily dependent on Soviet aid and export income, led many to believe that the socialist island would soon follow suit. Cuba was set adrift, economically and ideologically, in a world that was marked by transitions to liberal democracy and the triumphalism of free-market capitalism. The Cuban government began a slow and painful process of extricating the country from the crisis. Over the decade of the 1990s, Cuba was reintegrated into global markets, tourism was expanded, and sectors such as the arts, sports, and medicine were harnessed to provide hard currency, all while the United States tightened the screws of the embargo in an attempt to hasten Cuba's demise.

In the end, Cuba once again defied the odds to survive, albeit in an altered form. The ongoing isolation of Cuba in a digital era and the desperate need for outlets of expression, combined with the high quality of Cuban arts education, state funding for culture, and the new ideas flowing into Cuban society, turned the island into a crucible that fostered all kinds of dynamic cultures. This collection of essays explores "the Cuban hustle," showing how ordinary Cubans have sought to create alternative cultures in the aftermath of the collapse of the Soviet Union. The Cuban hustle is part of a long history, dating back to the colonial era, of aspirations for social justice and the fashioning of modes of survival and expressive cultures that would be part of the long fight.

The idea of the hustle draws from contemporary Cuban vernacular, including the notions of *luchar*, *resolver*, *inventar*, and *jinetear*. This vocabulary has emerged to articulate the ways that Cubans negotiate the contradictions of everyday life in the post-Soviet era. Cubans have been forced to find creative strategies of survival, often depending on the black market. When hotel employees pilfer packets of butter from a breakfast buffet to sell on the black market, this is seen not as stealing but rather as *luchando* or struggling. Given the inflationary pressures that reduced the value of basic incomes, the cutbacks in welfare provisions, and a shortage of basic consumer items, Cubans cannot *buy* the goods and services they need; rather, they *resolve* them. This usually means procuring items on the black market or drawing on informal networks to find solutions. During the 1990s, the term *jinetear* or the act of *jineterismo* acquired the meaning of "hustling," but it referred to a much broader range of practices, including engaging in sex work, romantic relationships, or friendships with tourists. Another term that gained currency was *pingüino*—young Cuban males who exchanged sexual services with foreign men for money and consumer goods such as designer clothes. Cubans have invented alternative strategies, solutions, and work-arounds for daily survival and finding spaces of pleasure.

This spirit of creativity and imagination has been carried over into Cuban cultural life. Given the shortages of materials for art, music, and film, artists found new and original ways to make their art. Cuba's first hip hop DJ, Ariel Fernández, improvised a set of turntables with Walkmans as the decks. Without access to the internet, Cubans found ways to download and circulate material on flash drives in a phenomenon known as the Weekly Packet. In the search for spaces of cultural expression in the small provinces outside the city, artists took over abandoned factories and turned them into cultural centers. Conditions of scarcity have provided the impetus for a culture of spontaneous improvisation.

I first visited Cuba in 1998, curious to see what a socialist country looked like. I encountered a society marked by growing divisions of class, gender, and race. Practices such as sex work that were made redundant by the revolution had become visible once again. Those on state salaries were unable to make ends meet. There was a restless, discontent younger generation. Yet as I returned to Cuba over the years, I began to see how a seething undercurrent was regenerating Cuban social life with the development of feminist and antiracism movements, as well as vocal criticisms expressed within cultural movements such as documentary film and public art. I visited Cuba again at the end of 2017, about a year after Donald Trump was elected to office with an agenda to end rapprochement with Cuba and an open policy of confrontation and regime change. These essays cover that twenty-year period of Cuban history, documenting the sheer inventiveness of ordinary Cubans as they hustled not only to survive, but to create meaning in a time of turmoil.

For the most part, the Western media has been preoccupied with the idea of Cubans as trapped within a one-state autocracy, yearning for political and consumer freedoms unavailable to them. Cubans are generally depicted as repressed entrepreneurs: a world of small businesspeople, dissidents, bloggers, and others who want freedom of speech and freedom of commerce. The progression of Cuban society is its journey toward capitalism, the evolution of Cubans to become more like us. All of this betrays a deep failure to understand Cuba on its own terms. There are many trajectories and models that loom large in the worldviews of Cubans, from the black radical tradition in the United States to the model of Chinese market socialism and the Pink Tide revolutions that swept Latin America. Some want more space to speak out critically or engage in commercial activities. And the growing presence of corporations such as Airbnb and Netflix is fostering new capitalist rationalities. But we must also understand the ways that consciousness and modes of being are deeply interwoven with and shaped by values of collectivism, egalitarianism, and voluntarism, derived from the socialist and postindependence past.

These essays depict a society in transition, but not necessarily one that is moving in a unilinear direction toward an embrace of capitalism. Rather, they reveal a range of utopic and liberatory visions that often take a socialist worldview as the horizon of the taken-for-granted, while also reflecting the multiple influences that have come to play a role in Cuban society from antiracist, anticapitalist, feminist, and LGBTQ movements to open source information sharing, gamer culture, rock, hip hop, and reggae.

The dismantling of the Soviet Union, with its oversized influence over Cuban society, created the space for a range of groups to assert themselves in the post-Soviet period. This groundswell of self-organized cultural and activist movements presented a new challenge for the Cuban government. While the government could find ways to manage and collaborate with emerging actors, in other respects they presented a deep challenge to existing orthodoxies. Hence we see the dance of promotion and deflection, sponsorship and censorship that marks the relationship of these movements with the Cuban state in the post-Soviet era.

There is an emphasis in these essays on antiracist movements in Cuba and particularly forms of black cultural expression such as hip hop and visual arts. Among the inequalities that became more visible during the 1990s, racialized poverty was at the fore. This was particularly glaring in a society that had at its core the promise of lifting up the most marginalized and eliminating racism. As black Cubans were more likely to be stuck in the stagnant state sector, with few opportunities or capital for setting up small businesses and little access to the tourism industry, they began to see once again the need for independent self-organization. The critiques were first articulated in cultural forms such as hip hop, by black youth who felt shut out from both the gains of the revolution and the promises of the new Cuba. Through the period of normalization and into the contemporary period, black Cubans have asserted their demands of inclusion and equality.

The second decade of the new millennium has been a time of historic and unprecedented changes in US-Cuban relations, from the resuming of diplomatic relations between the two countries under Barack Obama, the first visit of a US president to the island in nearly a century, and the death of the larger-than-life leader Fidel Castro to the reintroduction of travel restrictions, sanctions, and removal of embassy staff under Donald Trump. Under the Trump administration, there is the ongoing threat of foreign intervention and covert attempts to undermine Cuba's sovereignty. But as the closing essays attest, even these moves cannot undo the ongoing collaborations between grassroots groups in both countries and the pursuit of local community projects based in ideals of social justice.

PART I

CULTURES OF THE SPECIAL PERIOD

The severe economic crisis in Cuba that followed the collapse of the Soviet Union led the Cuban state to declare a "special period in times of peace" in September 1990. This euphemism, intended to minimize the expected duration of the difficulties, was adapted from a contingency plan that had been devised by the state in case of a military attack. During the worst of the special period in the early to mid-1990s, there were widespread shortages, a drastic deterioration in living standards, frequent blackouts, and a rise in unemployment. This state of economic crisis, which lasted through the period of the 1990s and new millennium, was alleviated for some who managed to integrate themselves into a new tourism- and remittance-based economy, while others continued to suffer its effects. Cubans emerged from the darkest days, but they did so unequally, leading one art critic to quip that "the Special Period is more special for some than for others."

The onset of the special period had a marked impact on the arts. The period of the 1980s had been one of experimentation and critical art, with artists pushing the boundaries of what was acceptable. Visual artists made art that directly took on state orthodoxies and often confronted head-on with bureaucrats. Filmmakers created collectives such as Grupo Nos-y-Otros to democratize film production. Artists took on taboo themes and faced censorship from the government, but important cultural figures such as the minister Marcia Leiseca and filmmaker Tomás Gutiérrez Alea advocated for them with the authorities.

This moment of openness came to a crashing halt after the collapse of the Soviet Union, when the country lost billions of dollars in Soviet aid and export income. Artists and galleries found themselves without basic supplies for producing art and for exhibitions. There was a recession in the film industry as funding was not available for production. The government took on a siege mentality, clamping down on forms of critical expression. The film *Alicia en el Pueblo de las Maravillas* (Alice in Wondertown), produced by Daniel Díaz Torres during the years of critical experimentation, was released in 1991 and banned after four days in theaters. This section presents an interview I carried out with the filmmaker, where he describes the vilification of his film and the way it reflected the climate of repression and censorship that marked the early years of the special period. It was a moment of silence in the arts during which many artists left Cuba.

By the mid-1990s, Cuba had started to come out of the crisis of the special period through increased reliance on tourism, foreign investment, and remittances from Cubans abroad. The arts were also resuscitated through their integration into new global networks of production and distribution. The entrance of the global market had multiple and contradictory effects within Cuban culture. In addition to providing basic resources and materials for artists, filmmakers, and musicians, the fetishization of difference as a marketable commodity for global consumers opened new possibilities for artists to address themes of race, sexuality, and gender in their work. At the same time, new market conditions of production prompted a greater emphasis on individualism, the commercialization of art that would appeal to collectors and tourists, and a focus by artists on their personal careers rather than activism or collective experimentation.

Transnational networks also reshaped the Cuban cultural sphere. From the annual Havana Biennial, which brought artists and collectors from around the world, to the influence of NGOs and women's organizations and the impact of American hip hop culture, Cubans were opened up to a vast range of new ideas and practices. Particularly given the rise of racial and gender inequalities as a result of Cuba's insertion into a global market economy, transnational networks provided a language for speaking about feminism, gender, black identity, and racism. The mid-1990s saw the formation of the Cuban feminist network Magín (Image), which brought together women communications professionals who organized around issues of gender. In this period, young black Cubans also created a local hip hop movement that provided a vocal assertion of black identity. For the first time in the history of the revolution, an independent feminist organization and critical cultures existed outside of state-sanctioned forms of expression.

As the Cuban state had started once again to consolidate itself through foreign partnerships and earnings from tourism, it also began to rein in some of these critical cultural and social movements. In 1996–97, there was a bureaucratic offensive during which the political leadership dissolved the nongovernmental research center Centro de Estudios Sobre América (CEA), arrested over a dozen leaders of the umbrella group Cuban Council, and dissolved Magín. In keeping with a longer-term strategy toward Afro-Cuban cultures, the state began to incorporate and co-opt the Cuban hip hop movement. It created a hip hop agency led by rappers and sponsored an annual hip hop festival.

The result was a reshaping of the engagement between artists and the state. In place of the openly confrontational art of the 1980s, artists and activists now sought to negotiate with state officials and penetrate state organizations. A new generation of visual artists, rap musicians, feminists, and filmmakers created expressive cultures based in practices of collective participation, working in public spaces, and taking on taboo themes. As a consequence of their exposure to the market, these actors also expanded their critiques from the Cuban state to the global market and tourist economy. The lens of their work broadened to take up gendered and racialized representations in the media, the rise of sex tourism, and growing inequality and individualism in Cuban society.

The vibrant cultural production and activism of the special period went on to nurture future generations and projects that would take root in the new millennium. Artists who went abroad brought back novel influences to Cuban society. The older generation of feminist activists become mentors to younger women who carried on their legacy.

Revolution and Rumba

Cuba in the Special Period

I spent my first days in Havana walking down the broad, tree-lined streets of el Vedado, going past stores with long queues but little on the shelves. I passed Cuban women in tight Lycra clothing who were hanging onto the arms of white tourists. They were known as *jineteras*, the term meaning "jockey," used to refer to street hustlers and sex workers. Children followed me, selling flowers or T-shirts to earn dollars. I paused outside the famous Coppelia ice-cream parlor, which had closed for repairs six months earlier but showed no signs of opening again. As I walked through Old Havana, the crumbling buildings seemed to reflect the decay and stasis that pervaded the city.

Was this the reality of the special period, as Cubans continued to suffer under the economic embargo imposed by the United States?

Havana was getting me down, so when my friend Norma called and asked if I'd like to spend a few days with her friend, the famous Afro-Cuban sculptor Agustín Drake, in the neighboring province of Matanzas, I accepted.

As I got off the bus in the quaint town, I wondered what the house of a famous sculptor would look like. Shortly, I arrived at the address, a terrace house. I went to knock on the enormous wooden door, but then I saw a short man in paint-splattered overalls, the handyman perhaps, busy painting the outside of the house.

"Excuse me, but does Agustín Drake live here?"

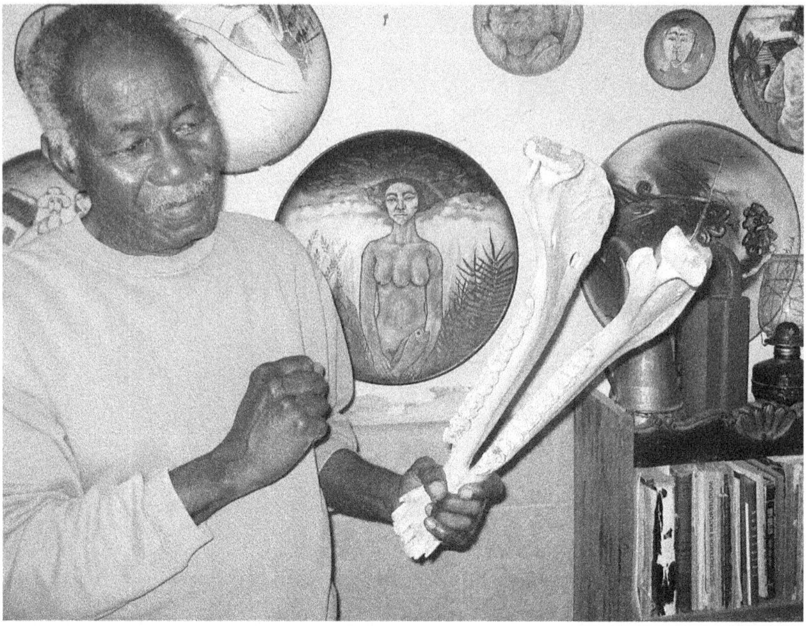

Figure 1.1 Agustín Drake. Photo by the author.

The man chuckled to himself and, wiping his hand on his overalls, extended it to me.

"Let me introduce myself. I am Drake."

I blushed, but Drake continued. "Before the revolution, I wasn't recognized as a sculptor, so while I was doing my art I had to learn house painting to earn my daily keep. But I guess the skill of house painting comes in handy now."

As he led me into his house, I noticed photos proudly exhibited on the walls: Drake as a young man at his art exhibition in Havana, Drake in the Soviet Union with Soviet artists, and Drake shaking hands with Fidel.

"It was only after the revolution of 1959 that my art was displayed in galleries," he told me. "I was given national recognition through government prizes and eventually sent overseas to represent Cuba."

The back room was his workroom, crammed with rocks, shells, stones, flowers, plants, and skins of all different hues, shapes, and textures. His only tools were ancient wooden cutting and pressing devices and pliers that transformed his raw materials into intricate sculptures of orichas, deities in Santería religion.

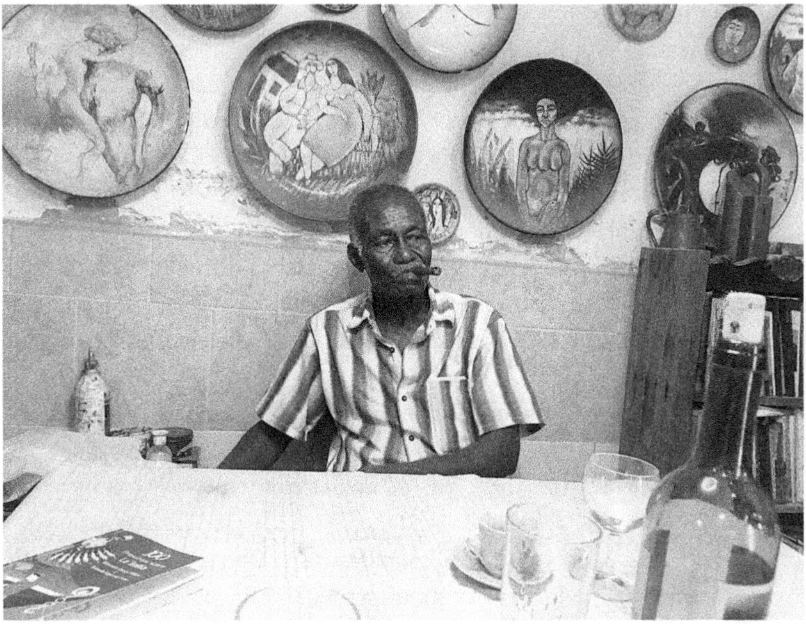

Figure 1.2 Agustín Drake. Photo by the author.

"Now I make these sculptures to sell to tourists in Varadero so that I can earn dollars," said Drake. "It's very different from the kind of art I was doing twenty years ago."

Drake pulled out an old, dusty album and handed it to me. There were sculptures of figures in heavy white-and-black clay, Cuba before the revolution. Then there were sculptures in all shades of clay. Drake told me that this was his vision of a society where the world was not divided into black and white, where color no longer mattered because the two colors had mixed and the world was populated with all shades of ochres and browns. These ideas of the mixed-race nation had been promoted not just by the Cuban Revolution, but by states across Latin America since the dawn of independence.

We sat down to talk over cups of thick, strong Cuban coffee. Drake asked me my impressions of Cuba, and I blurted out my response: "It's so different from what I had pictured. The only place where you can hear Cuban music is in the big clubs and hotels, which are off-limits to ordinary Cubans. Artists and musicians can only survive by catering to the tourist industry, like you yourself told me. And there seems to be so much poverty, most of it among black people."

"Unfortunately, things are changing with the increasing reliance on tourism," said Drake. "But if you want to understand more about Cuban society, don't rely on surface impressions. Go out and talk to ordinary Cuban people."

In the evening, I went for a walk by myself along the bay. Deep in my own thoughts, I lost track of time, and by the time I started back toward the city, it had already started to get dark.

As I approached the town, the hazy outlines of buildings and maze of streets didn't correspond with anything I remembered from the morning. I realized that I had forgotten to take Drake's address with me. Stopping two young women on the street, I asked, "Do you know where a famous sculptor Agustín Drake lives?"

The women giggled and nudged one another. "Yes," one answered. "If you like, we can take you to his house."

As we walked back into the town, the women chattered away, asking me all about life in Australia, and then I asked them about life in Matanzas.

They told me about their families and careers. One of them, María, was a violin teacher at the local institute of music, and the other, Leticia, was a ballerina.

I asked them how they survived under the dual dollar/peso economy. The legalization of the US dollar alongside the devalued Cuban peso had developed in the early 1990s as a strategy to help the economy recover. María said, "Without dollars, it is difficult. We earn only in Cuban pesos. We can't afford nice perfume, or nice clothes or makeup. But we can buy food in the markets in pesos."

The two women flirted with men on the streets, winking provocatively and carrying on a playful banter.

"Let's have some pizza and milkshakes," Leticia suggested.

"But I don't see any pizzerias around here," I said.

The local pizza spot wasn't immediately obvious, tucked away in someone's house. I noticed that there were dozens of these "pizzerias" along the street.

We had a filling meal of hot pizza, which was doughy bread with a strong cheese on top, and washed it down with batidos, milkshakes of cantaloupe, crushed ice, and milk. Groups of people stood around talking, smoking cigars, and enjoying the evening.

When I woke up the next morning, Drake was dressed in a collared shirt. He told me that he had planned to take me out for the day. Luckily I hadn't tried to imagine what the car of a famous sculptor would look like. When we walked outside, there was a small, brown, rust-covered, box-like mobile. It was handy that the windows were big enough to jump through, because the doors didn't work.

We drove in Drake's car through a jumble of pebble-lined streets to an old building. As we climbed the stone steps, I could hear the pounding of rumba rhythms. Inside was a six-piece group of percussionists, playing to a group of nearly twenty dancers.

"They are the original Muñequitos of Matanzas," Drake whispered as we took our seats at the front of the empty auditorium. "They rehearse here every day."

The dancers stood in a row, their knees bent, shoulders hunched over. Electric currents moved through their bodies, from the base of their spines to their necks and fingertips, as they undulated with the rapid, precise drumbeats.

I watched entranced as they formed a circle. A man and a woman moved into the center, sparring as the man tried playfully to touch the woman's pelvic area. She teased him and twisted out of his reach each time. The atmosphere in the room was charged with catcalls, whooping shouts, and the hypnotic energy of the congas and the claves.

Drake wanted to leave after an hour, and I reluctantly got up and left with him, my heart still full of the drums and the rhythms.

We got back into the car and drove around the lower reach of the city. Drake stopped at a number of houses, showing me where particular musicians had met to rehearse and how each distinct rumba style had originated with different networks of urban black musicians. The rumba sounds I was hearing were the products of generations of evolution and development, a synthesis of styles and lived experiences.

From the lower part of the city, he took me to the upper part and showed me the Instituto de Artes, where he had been the director for many years. From the roof of the institute, he pointed out his house, the building where we had gone for the rumba performance, and the local church.

"See how different it all looks from up here," he said.

Driving up to the small chapel on the hill was quite an effort for the little car, but wheezing and puffing, it managed to get there. From the top of the hill, the view of the whole town was immense. Again he pointed out his house, the building of the rumba performance, and the church, but also the Instituto de Artes and the upper part of the city where we had just been.

"When you are in one particular place, you can't see some things," he said. "Often just by moving, your vision clears."

The next day, I said farewell to Drake. I stood on the major highway and stuck out my thumb. I made my way back to Havana by *botella*, the system of travel which requires cars, by law, to take hitchhikers.

I passed fields and billboards of Che and Fidel and reflected on my time in Matanzas. Drake had showed me the city, how it is the product of contradictory forces, how it has evolved historically, and how we can see it from many different perspectives. But he also wanted me to understand Cuba in this way, and he showed me the dangers of a blinkered vision.

Note

An earlier version of this essay in a different form appeared in *Green Left Weekly*, August 13, 1998.

Alice in Wondertown

Interview with Filmmaker Daniel Diáz Torres

Daniel Diáz Torres was a Cuban film director and screenwriter who directed sixteen films before his death in 2013. He was the director of a highly controversial film, *Alicia en el pueblo de las Maravillas* (Alice in Wondertown), released in 1991. The film is a satirical comedy about a drama coach, Alicia, who goes to a small town called Maravillas for her obligatory year of community service. Maravillas is a parody of socialist bureaucracy, corruption, and mismanagement, where official discourse functions as Orwellian doublespeak. Cloudy drinking water is declared to be clear. The Sanatorium for Active Therapy and Neurology (SATAN) is advertised on television as "a model of devoted patient care." Signs such as "Congratulations, we've reached our target" follow scenes of corruption. Everyone in the town parrots the official newspeak, and the scatological imagery contributes to a sense of the characters' evasions and hypocrisy.

After just four days in theaters, the Cuban authorities recalled the film, and it was the target of a vicious media campaign in Cuba. I met with Diáz Torres in 2001 to discuss his experiences making film in Cuba and the reasons why his film met with the critical reaction that it did. In some ways, the response was emblematic of the broader cultural climate engendered by the collapse of the Soviet Union and the onset of the special period.

SUJATHA FERNANDES: How did you enter into the world of film? What made you interested in creating cinema?

DANIEL DIÁZ TORRES: When I was an adolescent, twelve or thirteen years old, I loved going to the movies. In those years, 1961, 1962, we practically only had movies from socialist countries. But then in 1963 and 1964, the Cuban Film Institute [Instituto Cubano del Arte y Industria Cinematográficos, ICAIC] began to promote a richer programming with films such as *Meridiana*, movies of Fellini. This got me interested in cinema.

I got my start as the subdirector of Latin American news, along with Santiago Álvarez, Rolando Díaz, and Fernando Pérez. Together, we edited between eighty and one hundred news editions. A news report was practically a weekly documentary, with very open themes, and that was how I learned to make cinema. I worked there for four years. I was interested in documentary, but I was even more interested in fiction.

My first work was connected to my experiences with the literacy campaign in 1961. I was in Escambray, and I worked with Manuel Pérez on *El hombre de Maisinicú* (The man from Maisinicú). This was my first film. But we had reached a violent moment of class struggle at that time, a small counterrevolutionary war in this mountainous zone.

After that, I began to work in fiction. I like comedy, humor. It's how I see reality. It's never about derision, nor that we don't take things seriously. Rather the opposite. When we use humor, when we use irony, we have the possibility to reflect on everything that we're seeing. We can see it with more distance, which helps with our analysis of certain situations. I think that the master of humor, Charlie Chaplin, is a comedian, but he also has moments of profound emotion.

FERNANDES: *Alicia* was produced by a film collective that you founded, called Grupo Nos-y-Otros. How did the group come together? How did it operate in the production of films?

DIÁZ TORRES: *Alicia* was the only film that we made. I was the director of the group. It was a small group of young people of university level. They were influenced by comedy, theater, black humor, and they were writing original works. This period of the 1980s was very rich in the cultural sphere and gave rise to a flourishing of visual arts, theater, and literature. After *Alicia*, the group continued working as comedy writers, and then later they dissolved. Some of them work in magazines, some are musicians, but others continued as scriptwriters and writers. The only collective experience we had as a group was with *Alicia*.

FERNANDES: I would like to talk about your film *Alicia*. How do you explain the strong reaction to *Alicia* in the Cuban media? In interviews, you discuss various reasons, for example, the interpretation of the film as socialist realism, the sense of culpability that people interpreted as an accusation, and so on. But why was this film so controversial and not others like *La vida es silbar* (Life is to whistle) and *Fresa y chocolate* (Strawberry and chocolate), which were also very critical?

DIÁZ TORRES: I think it is important to contextualize it. At the end of the 1980s, we had confronted a series of events, including at the international level. The Soviet Union had entered into crisis; it seemed as though we were going to see positive changes within socialism, such as perestroika. It signified a break with all of the codified language, with the schematism and propaganda. I think that perestroika and the changes that were approved in that moment, in 1986, 1987 and 1988, really carried the hope of a renewal within the stasis that the Soviet Union had fallen into. Young people most of all had grown tired of the ideological and media rhetoric and propaganda of Soviet socialism.

And I think that happened in Cuba as well, a chance to pull ourselves out of the stasis. For the first time, people were dying to buy the latest magazines from Moscow. And part of this was the so-called Rectification of Errors and Negative Tendencies in Soviet socialism. We saw that from our own perspective—the necessity of rectification of errors, confronting problems head-on. This climate nurtured the idea of our film in 1988.

Fidel himself defended the right to take risks and make errors, as important factors in what makes a revolution. If the revolution had been restrained, careful, waiting for the best moments, there wouldn't have been a revolution. If we had always followed the rules in the manuals of communism, there would have been no revolution. No attack at Moncada, no disembarking from the *Granma*, nothing like this.

But unfortunately, this didn't continue. I believe that a society has to be in a permanent process of change, renewal, overcoming. Because otherwise we remain in stasis. Even though we're talking about questions of politics and ideology, this also influences aesthetics and what artists do. I think that this climate of openness went from 1985 to 1988. So what happened? It wasn't a Hollywood happy ending. Soviet society was much more deteriorated and broken than we had thought. Here we had always seen it through rose-colored glasses. The result was that bam, bam, bam, it imploded completely, much to the surprise of the North Americans.

I think that Soviet society collapsed due to its own internal contradictions, dogmatism, its failure to be a truly revolutionary society. The phenomenon of perestroika and glasnost ended curiously, as if they had accelerated the process of deterioration. For example, you say, "I have to fix my house, it has cracks." But when you start to fix the roof, it turns out that all the beams are broken and the house collapses in on itself. Something similar happened in the Soviet Union. It was not able to be fixed.

I give you all of this context because this is the context in which the film was made. What happened between writing the script of the movie and the release of the movie was that the world as we knew it ended. The movie was released in 1991, following the crisis of the Socialist Bloc, the end of the Soviet Union, the whole process of self-destruction.

My hope was that the movie would question all of the negative elements within our society, bureaucratic tendencies, conformism, opportunism, duplicity. Unfortunately, there is a propagandistic facade that everybody has revolutionary consciousness, and it's not like that because life is not like that. Things are complex. People have many necessities in their daily life. These feed duplicity when people have needs that they have to resolve here or there, that sometimes emerge as small illegalities. All this forms part of a daily modus vivendi which contradicts the grand words that saturate the political sphere. There is oversaturation; the repetition of propaganda ends up generating its opposite. I don't think they have learned this lesson. It continues and, well, these are the things that the film *Alicia* criticizes.

What happened? The film came out in 1991. The socialist camp had disappeared; the island was desperately isolated as the North American embargo was tightened. There was a sentiment of being a besieged fortress, of uncertainty at the level of the party, by the leaders of the country. They felt that the movie contained a level of unacceptable criticism. Some even called it counterrevolutionary. If the movie had come out in 1988 or the beginning of 1989, it would have been different. I think that the reaction by the authorities, by the party, was out of proportion.

But I think that although it was a very unfortunate moment, it helped to spark a debate. Eighteen of the most important Cuban directors, including Titón [Tomás Gutiérrez Alea], Santiago Álvarez, and Humberto Solás, met with the party leadership and debated these problems, very seriously. It emerged that a law had been proposed to dissolve ICAIC. Upon hearing of this law, the artists questioned it. I think that the politicians understood that in the terrain of art and culture, things are much more complex. You can't see them in the same way as political conjunctures. An artwork shouldn't be seen through an exclusively political lens. For their part, the filmmakers understood the complexity of the political moment that had passed. None of us could have had the foresight to predict what would happen.

The eclectic form of the film, with its satirical tone, elements of black humor, and irony, reflects a certain Caribbean vision of our problems. Some people compared the work to [George Orwell's] *1984*. I said no, *1984* is a serious, gray, sad society. That is not what is in this movie. We can see negative things shown in the film, but it doesn't end on a depressing note. At the end, the character of Alicia makes an announcement calling for nonconformism.

I had hoped that the film would give rise to a debate, a discussion, a polemic. The objective of the film was that each one would reach their own conclusions. Some of the main problems came from the belief that the character who directs the sanatorium was Fidel Castro. This seems reductive to me. I was portraying a concept about bureaucratic power, impersonal power. Fidel may be a controversial personality whom many see as a caudillo. But that is not related to the characters I represent in this film. To reduce the problems of Cuba, the good and the bad, is unacceptable, and it's not what I'm expressing in this film.

The film was appropriated by different political interests. Each side used it to reinforce their own position. In Cuba, the film was censored and banned from the cinema after four days alongside a negative media campaign. Unfortunately the film made it to Miami, and some in Miami took advantage of the conflicts produced by the film to bolster their position.

This was all a distraction, a vilification of the film where nobody saw it in its original state. People invented scenes of the movie that didn't exist. There was a proliferation of rumor, of highly speculative interpretations. All of this produced a sociological phenomenon connected with the uncertainty of the start of the special period. These were moments where it was predicted that the revolution would last only two or three years. All this climate inevitably led to an abnormal reception of the film, one that was amplified and hyperbolized. We have to see it in this context, but this doesn't excuse those who promoted such a disproportionate response.

Some people say that censorship is typical of the revolution, but that's not true. ICAIC was never directed by censorship or by bureaucrats. There was Alfredo Guevara, a man of culture and central to the cultural life of the revolution. Afterward came Julio García Espinosa, film director, script writer, poet, who then became director of the Book Institute [Instituto de Libros]. We never had a colonel, a functionary installed by the party. I'm not trying to idealize the situation. There is a sea of contradictions. There has never been a serious analysis of the controversy sparked by *Alicia*. Everything became so extremely politicized, which was followed by a vilification of the film as if it were a project designed to attack the revolution in its weakest moment.

This was not a film that was made clandestinely. It was in production for a long time. The script was there, and everyone could read it. When the criticisms emerged, there was a lack of faith in the artists. Anyone could have called me to discuss it, and they didn't. The decision to withdraw the film, the whole media campaign, there was never any debate about it. Rather, the film was just knocked down. That was what bothered me the most.

Many people said to me that if this had happened in East Germany, the director would have been jailed or exiled. In this case, none of that happened. It was unfortunate. No one makes a movie to face this kind of fury. I believe that all of us who worked on this movie, we did it with our best intentions as revolutionaries. We wanted to speak about phenomena like opportunism, duplicity, using humor. For me, humor is an essential quality of intelligence. In a good joke, we can see the contradictions of reality. This is my vision. I don't want to impose it on anybody.

FERNANDES: You have said that the objective of the film was to provoke people to think critically, following the vision of film directors such as Tomás Gutiérrez Alea and Julio García Espinosa. Do you think that you achieved this?

DÍAZ TORRES: Yes, I think the film was important. When they talk about Cuban cinema, this film is not often discussed. In articles about Cuban film of the 1990s, some people say that the problem with the film is that it was not good. This seems to be a bit false to me. It allows them to dismiss the film because of its poor quality. I do think that the film created certain elements of reflection that allowed other films like *Fresa y chocolate* to emerge. I think that it helped create a calmer climate, more mature, in order to bring into focus problems of cinema, art, and culture. The political leadership came to understand these things, and the film also helped to facilitate a level of self-reflection in many creators. I think it was mutually beneficial, despite the fact that what happened was traumatic.

I continue to have this critical view. Some people say that the response to the film was excessive because the film itself was excessive. I say that it was deliberately excessive. I think that the film could have had a space that was generated by the film itself. But its reception was totally exceptionalized by the groups of militants sent to the cinemas in omnibuses. The film could have been just a film, whose importance within Cuban cinema could be determined in aesthetic and other terms. There were a few serious reviews of the film, not because they spoke positively about the film. But these were not published—because the media was only interested in the attacks. While the film was very popular and attractive to the people, all of those writing about it were critical of it. Even today there are a ton of copies of the film in this country. People have the movie, I don't know how they got it, clandestinely, and it is a movie that has become a myth. Or rather, the mythification of the film has been a product of this situation.

FERNANDES: How would you describe the state of Cuban cinema in the 1990s? Do you think that the revolution has developed an active and critical cinema public?

DÍAZ TORRES: I believe that in the 1960s and 1970s, there was a programming with much better possibilities, which helped to create a much richer public. It is certain that in the special period it became more difficult to obtain copies of movies to be able to show them. Earlier there would be three or four weekly showings. What became more popular with the youth was video, and in video we get the worst of American cinema. Here in this country, it's incredible that although these videos are not sold in stores, there are hundreds of thousands of them in circulation. There has been an impoverishment of taste. It's not the same public as in the 1960s and 1970s. But what excites me is that when the festival of cinema comes around, over the course of two weeks more than three hundred thousand people go to see a variety of films, and the cinemas are packed. What I like about the public here is that they can see a bad film, after which they'll watch a soap opera that could be very mediocre, but they still have the capacity to appreciate a film with a different aesthetic level. All of this exists; the public here has this complexity.

Magín

Feminist Organizing in Cuba

Feminist organizing was one of the first kinds of collective organizing to emerge during the special period. This is not surprising given the impact and burden of this period on women. In the mid-1990s, women communications professionals in Cuba started meeting informally to discuss issues related to gender such as growing sex tourism, the gender gap, and representations of women in the media. They came together to form a feminist organization known as Magín, or Image. Up until this point, the official Federation of Cuban Women (FMC) had been the primary advocate for women's issues in Cuba. But as Cuban society underwent structural changes as a result of its integration into a market economy, the FMC was unequipped to deal with the new problems that were arising.

At the same time, as Cuba reintegrated into a global economy, Cuban women had more contact with feminist groups in Latin America and internationally. Magín was formed through these encounters with feminists in international meetings and through participation in transnational activist circles. Transnational networks created new avenues for feminist activism in Cuba, while at the same time limiting the scope of the movement. International conferences and possibilities of networking made available new ideas and resources for local organizing. But the elitist nature of international events and the demands of networking led to the growing professionalization of an emerging feminism on the island. The priorities and funding constraints of international bodies posed risks to the nascent Cuban movement by narrowing the broad range of issues that activists from Magín had originally sought to address. Although the organization was eventually closed down by the Cuban state, it did create new spaces for dialogue and feminist activism in Cuban society.

Gender Relations and the Special Period

The collapse of the Soviet Union and the economic reforms of the special period had specific, gendered effects within Cuba. Women shouldered the burdens of a pared-down welfare state because of their responsibility for household tasks. There was an increase in sex work, or *jineterismo*, as women looked for opportunities to supplement their meager incomes in the informal sector. Black women faced higher levels of poverty and were especially concentrated in this informal sector. There was a rise in attitudes of machismo. As Cuba was marketed globally to attract tourism and investment, images of black women as erotic and sexually available became more common, especially in tourism brochures and magazines such as *Sol y son* (Sun and son).

Upon coming to power in 1959, the Cuban revolutionary leadership had promoted the idea that women would be liberated from sexual oppression through their participation in the workforce. The FMC was established to educate women and eliminate practices such as sex work. It proceeded on the assumption that the revolution had ended patriarchy. By the early 1970s, the Cuban leadership realized that sex discrimination had not been eradicated. In 1975, the bill known as the Family Code legislated that men and women should share equally the responsibilities of household maintenance and childcare.

For the first three decades of the Cuban Revolution, some fairly dramatic changes occurred in the lives of women, including an increase in female employment and education, declining rates of poverty, and a reduction in sex work and illiteracy. These changes were driven by an active mobilization of women in the early postrevolutionary period.[1] Such changes in Cuban society continued to structure the entry of Cuba into a global market system, reducing the severity of social inequalities and cushioning women from drastic change. To some extent, the relative successes of the Cuban Revolution in promoting gender equality and the gender-blind nature of official discourse had reduced the incentive of women to mobilize as feminists. But by the time the special period hit, women were feeling the gendered effects of the crisis and were looking for ways to organize.

The Influence of Transnational Networks

As a network of professional women active in issues of media and communications, Magín gained impetus from the growth in transnational organizing, conferences, and networking that began in the 1980s. Representatives from feminist and women's groups across Latin America met in various regional meetings or *encuentros*. International public events such as the Fourth World Conference on Women (FWCW) in Beijing and an alternative NGO forum held in the small town of Huairou, China, in 1995, and later the World Social Forum in 2001, held in Porto Alegre, Brazil, provided the catalyst for new perspectives on gender and feminism in Cuba. Representatives of the FMC began attending the regional meetings in 1987, but it was not until the 1999 meeting in Juan Dolio that non-FMC activists attended from Cuba.

One of the features of transnational organizing has been the formation of issue networks. In 1993, the Iberoamerican Women and Communications Network formed and held its first conference in Havana. The conference was attended by a group of female communications professionals who heard topics related to gender being discussed for the first time. The idea that gender differences are socially constructed and not innate properties deriving from biology was a radical insight for those present at the forum. The women decided that they needed a Cuban organization distinct from the FMC to address issues related to gender and communications. In 1994, the group Magín, meaning "image," "mind," or "imagination," was formed among Cuban communications workers. The large number of women working in the Cuban communications sector gave impetus to the project.

The women of Magín, who were baptized *margineras* by Brazilian feminist Cristina Cavalcanti, sought to establish themselves as an official organization. They formed an organizing committee consisting of fifteen communications professionals working in different fields. The newly constituted organization applied to the Cuban state for NGO status but did not receive it. Nevertheless, Magín was supported by the FMC because the women initially distanced themselves from feminism.[2] The FMC had traditionally seen itself as a feminine, not feminist, organization. Because of the stigma attached to feminism in Cuban society, the magineras had to find alternative ways of framing their project.

The women made practical use of the theoretical frameworks offered by international actors, talking about gender rather than directly about feminism. According to Magín member Norma Guillard, "Gender as a category of analysis and transformation was more easily assimilated. It didn't carry a negative connotation as a word." In later years, it also became beneficial for women to use the term "gender" in funding proposals to international organizations, given its currency in those circles. The women did not intend for gender to remain a purely analytical category. For Guillard, the task of Magín was to introduce the concept of gender and connect it to an idea of feminism that could be associated with a project for liberation. By framing their project in terms of gender and gradually reintroducing the idea of feminism, the magineras avoided alienating people from their project and were able to win support from various sectors.

Magín activists sought to provide alternative channels for discussion about issues of gender. They instituted a program of development, whereby they set their goals and projects for the year. Guillard, who kept the records of the organization, notes that Magín had about 385 members in Havana, with smaller groups of about twenty members each in the provinces of Pinar del Río and Santiago de Cuba. Each time Magín held workshops or forums it attracted between thirty-five and sixty people who were generally, but not always, communications professionals. Since Magín had few resources for publicity, it had to rely mainly on unofficial networks of friends, family, and colleagues to pass on information.

Magín met on Fridays to debate various themes, including sexism in language, racial imagery in the media, women and change, and female subjectivity in film.[3] It released Number 0 of a journal, *Magín*, which, due to high production costs, was the only edition ever produced. The activists of Magín also organized workshops dealing with broader, more politically provocative themes, such as "Jineterismo and Prostitution" and "What's Happening with Civil Society in Cuba?" Through their meetings, workshops, and publications, supported in part by donations from international organizations, the women of Magín were able to reach a limited but important constituency within Cuba.

Many of the founding members of Magín became key players in regional movements and networks to promote gender awareness in the media and to challenge negative stereotypes and images of women. Two leaders of Magín travelled to Brazil in 1994. Guillard participated in a forum of publicists in Rio de Janeiro, and Niurka Pérez Rojas presented a paper at the Federal University of Rio de Janeiro. Magín maintained close contact with networks of communications professionals in other countries, such as the Dominican feminist network of journalists, Primera Plana, and a female communications group in Mexico known as CIMAC. In 1995, Magín brought together women from Argentina, Brazil, Venezuela, Colombia, El Salvador, Guatemala, Bolivia, and Cuba for a conference on women in communications. The conference participants decided to create a network for the circulation of information, such as articles, videos, and graphics by and about women. The network, called Imagen, would be based in Havana with a redistribution point in Brazil.

Transnational connections clearly benefited the Cuban feminists of Magín, providing them with new theoretical perspectives and financial resources, as well as boosting their legitimacy within Cuba. Solidarity networks represented by grassroots organizations, such as the New York–based human rights group Madre and the women's group Sister and Sister from Washington, DC, paid visits to Magín, bringing them medicines, paper, food, and other resources for their workshops. There was also a more official international presence with such groups as the United Nations Children's Fund (UNICEF), the UN Development Program (UNDP), the UN Development Fund for Children (UNIFEM), and the relief agency OXFAM. These organizations offered Magín more financial resources and a larger international profile. For instance, Magín received some start-up funds from OXFAM, which allowed them to purchase their first photocopier. Most of Magín's meetings were held in the Havana offices of the Cuban Association of the United Nations (ACNU).

The decision of the Magín women to work within the media came partly from their own experiences in this profession. Since funding was available from international organizations for issues such as gender representations in the media, feminists also chose to focus on these issues in order to make themselves attractive to donors. But the women of Magín began with a more expansive notion of the media than what was proposed by international organizations. An anonymous member, interviewed by María López Vigil, claims, "In creating Magín we decided to begin through the media, but starting from a very broad concept of media. We didn't want only journalists, radio broadcasters, publicists.... We also began to bring in teachers. Who is a better multiplier of messages than them? And family doctors, who also multiply messages. And popular power representatives and academics and researchers."[4]

This broad concept of the media was always strong within Magín, but through engagement with official international donors, a notion of media as products for consumption began to gain currency in the organization. In 1995, Magín received financing from the OXFAM Regional Office of the Caribbean in order to begin a training program for the creation of communicative products with a gender focus.[5] The women of Magín adopted the concept of "communicative products" as a professional tool. As Guillard told me, "By communicative products, we mean that if you work in radio, musical programs, if you write novels or work in television, you should work with the perspective of gender.... When you create your product, it should be permeated with a gender focus." The objective of Magín was narrowed from building a movement that might have included a broader sector of people involved in education and communication to creating a professional tool for workers in the mass media.

The turn inward to questions of self-cultivation and self-esteem in Magín can also be attributed to the influence of transnational organizations. The change was partly a reaction to the exclusive focus by the FMC on gender equality as legal and economic equality. Individual identity and subjectivity had been submerged by focus on the collective over many years. The turn to the self was a tendency in Cuban society before international agencies arrived, but the agencies played an important role in shaping and promoting this particular orientation. In 1993, María Ester Mogollón, a specialist from a Peruvian NGO known as Centro Flora Tristan, carried out a training course in Cuba on "Self-Esteem and Feminism" for many of the women who were to form Magín. These kinds of courses by foreign specialists influenced Magín activists, who themselves conducted more than fifty workshops on "individual growth." In the workshops, one of the primary guides used was a manual designed by UNICEF, UNIFEM, and the Pan American Health Organization/World Health Organization (OPS/OMS) titled "Fostering Our Self-Esteem." Because Cuban women at this time were facing extraordinary conditions of hardship, these workshops functioned as support groups and spaces for catharsis. But by focusing on issues of self-esteem, foreign manuals and specialists encouraged women to devise individual solutions for confronting the crisis, rather than more collective solutions.

The need to appeal to transnational advocacy NGOs for funding encouraged greater professionalization of feminist activism within Magín. In their engagement with international agencies, local women's groups had to make themselves visible, since they were competing with other organizations for funding and resources. This usually meant emphasizing professional qualifications. In a form letter sent to various international organizations asking for funding to attend the Beijing conference, the members of Magín defined themselves as "highly trained professionals" and "highly qualified," emphasizing their influence within the media in Cuban society. Professionalization of the organization was also apparent in the training workshops that were organized for media workers. While the women of Magín originally sought to link gender analysis to a broader liberatory project, their work increasingly came to be seen in terms of "gender-sensitivity," as a skill that had to be taught by specialists.

Following international trends, women sought to gain entry into state institutions and official sites. In their publications, Magín drew on strategy documents from the 1994 Beijing women's conference that focused on the participation of women in the political sphere as an important objective. The women of Magín used their international contacts to gain entry into state media organizations, including such traditionally patriarchal and conservative institutions as the Cuban Institute of Radio and Television (ICRT). Members of Magín worked closely with state institutions for gender reforms. The incorporation of feminists into state institutions gave them a degree of control over such aspects as the representation of women in tourism and gender-specific programming.

The Closure of Magín

Despite its close ties with state institutions, Magín differed from the official women's organization, particularly over questions of jineterismo and sex work. The FMC had consistently upheld the official position that jineterismo was immoral and participated in government offensives against it. Vilma Espin, leader of the FMC, denounced *jineteras* as "decadent trash whose parents had lost control of them."[6] The women of Magín criticized the moral conservatism of the FMC. For example, Magín member and poet Georgina Herrera said, "The FMC has a completely bourgeois concept of moral values."[7] Instead, the margineras defended the rights of women to engage in jineterismo, as long as they retained their dignity and self-respect.

The independent stance that the magineras sought to take on various issues was a threat to the state, but the closure of Magín was more closely linked to the bureaucratic offensive of 1996–97. This offensive was spurred by a range of factors, including the limited economic recovery of the country, which put the Cuban state in a better position to reassume control over the provision of services; its reestablishment of trade links with a range of countries, which reduced the urgency of securing Western investments; internal adjustments resulting from the Fifth Party Congress of 1997; and the tightening of the US embargo, which increased the defensiveness of the political leadership.[8] The offensive included a crackdown on dissident organizations and independent groups. In February 1996, the Cuban government arrested more than a dozen leaders of the Cuban Council. On March 23 of that year, Raúl Castro gave a speech denouncing the activities of Cuban NGOs, independent organizations, and research groups, especially those that had relationships with foreign NGOs. This speech preempted the attacks that were to be launched against several groups, including Magín.

In September 1996, the Central Committee of the Communist Party of Cuba (PCC) called together its executive committee and the steering committee of Magín to dissolve the organization. According to one Magín member present at the meeting, the political leaders said that while the women's projects were valued, many people were being seduced by the enemy with scholarships and money, and that 70 percent of independent organizations were subversive in some way because foreign money was always given in exchange for political loyalties.[9] The leaders also claimed that Magín was duplicating other organizations such as the journalists' union and the FMC; such duplication is illegal in Cuba. The women disagreed. López Vigil, who was present at the meeting noted, "Magín's specific purpose was to change the image of women in the media by introducing the concept of gender, and by means of self-esteem workshops—things that nobody else was doing. They didn't accept that argument." López Vigil suspected that behind the claims of redundancy lay a deeper fear about women's potential for autonomy: "In Cuba, there's a real fear about duplicating organizations, but there is an even greater fear of women organizing independently."[10]

The party leaders concluded that an autonomous organization of women presented a risk of division to Cuban society and that in order to maintain national unity, it would have to disband. One member of Magín said, "It was clear that behind all the arguments was basically a *machista* line of thinking: 'You, naive little ladies, can be easily seduced by the enemy's bait, unaware that they want to buy you with money, with different ideas, and with individualism. We, big strong men, understand how politics works and must save you from temptation.'"[11] Although the claims were clearly unjustified, the women accepted the decision because they knew there were no other options if they did not want to be considered dissidents and have their professional lives in Cuba curtailed. The cordial nature of the meeting was partly due to the status of several prominent Magín leaders who were also PCC members, which may have protected the magineras from more open repression.

The closing down of Magín by the state ended a productive period of feminist activity in Cuba. Transnational influences had already encouraged the magineras to develop a narrowly focused professional association, rather than building a broad feminist movement. The women of Magín recognized this. Daisy Rubiera said, "I can't say that we were a feminist movement; we were only professional women in the media seeking more knowledge." According to Sonnia Moro, "The majority of Magín's members were professionals with experience and work." Guillard also noted, "Magín didn't have a force of broader change in its work. It was only about changing consciousness in ways that would influence the work you did." Goals of gender awareness and communication were largely focused on individual professional work.

Futures of Cuban Feminism

Transnationalism created new spaces for women to raise issues of feminism and gender in Cuban society. But the influence of transnational advocacy networks ultimately led to a further marginalizing of autonomous women's groups in relation to both state and society. Like developmentalist and socialist states in Asia, North Africa, and the Middle East, the monopoly exercised by the state over women's bureaus in Cuba reduced the space for independent feminist activity. Feminists who try to organize autonomously find themselves caught in a vicious cycle, vulnerable to state repression and reliant on small handouts from foreign donors that further marginalize their position within society.

In contexts where state institutions are unwilling to relinquish power to autonomous feminist groups, some feminists find it more productive to work within state-sanctioned organizations in order to build and develop their perspectives. In Tunisia during the 1990s, women found it easier to work within the official National Union of Tunisian Women (UNFT), which was able to reach a large number of women due to its structure and cadres.[12] Following liberalization in China, activists had more opportunities to demand organizational autonomy within the official women's bureau. But whether women decide to participate in official women's bureaus also depends on how open these structures are. Cuban feminists found the FMC highly resistant to change, so they chose to work within other state institutions. As director of the Cuban Society of Psychologists, Guillard started the Section on Identity, Diversity, and Social Communication in 2003. This section had an email list that reached groups and individuals internationally, and it organized regular events in Cuba in collaboration with the National Center for Sexual Education.

The women of Magín also sought to collaborate with young women in local cultural movements such as hip hop. The emergence of a feminist consciousness in Cuban hip hop shows that Magín was not an aberration in a context hostile to feminism. According to Guillard, "We cannot say that in Cuba we have a feminist movement, but there are many feminists in different organizations outside the FMC who have been inspired by this process of liberation. I think that Magín was an association of feminists who were discovering a liberating theory, and now each of its ex-members is fighting to create new spaces for feminism."

Sonnia Moro says, "Magín doesn't exist, but the magineras do."

Notes

An earlier version of this essay appeared in *Politics and Gender* 1, no. 3 (September 2005): 431–52.

1 Michelle Chase, *Revolution within the Revolution: Women and Gender Politics in Cuba, 1952-1962* (Chapel Hill: University of North Carolina Press, 2015).
2 Julie Shayne, *The Revolution Question: Feminisms in El Salvador, Chile, and Cuba* (New Brunswick, NJ: Rutgers University Press, 2004), 147.
3 Mirta Rodríguez Calderón, "Comunicadoras de Cuba: Fraguar alianzas para estrechar brechas de género," in ¡Di Mama! ¿Tú sabes qué cosa es género?, edited by Magín Comité Gestor (Havana: Magín Comité Gestor, 1996), 6–7.
4 María López Vigil, "Cuban Women's History: Jottings and Voices," *Envío* 17, no. 208 (1998): 41.
5 Rodríguez Calderón, "Comunicadoras de Cuba."
6 Cited in Coco Fusco, "Hustling for Dollars: *Jineterismo* in Cuba," in *Global Sex Workers: Rights, Resistance, and Redefinition*, edited by Kamala Kempadoo and Jo Doezema (New York: Routledge, 1998), 161.
7 Georgina Herrera, "Poetry, Prostitution, and Gender Esteem," in *Afro-Cuban Voices on Race and Identity in Contemporary Cuba*, edited by Pedro Pérez Sarduy and Jean Stubbs (Gainesville: University Press of Florida, 2000), 123.
8 Haroldo Dilla, "Larval Actors, Uncertain Scenarios, and Cryptic Scripts: Where is Cuban Society Headed?," in *Changes in Cuban Society since the Nineties*, edited by Joseph Tulchin and Ralph Espach (Boulder, CO: Rienner, 2005), 183–206.
9 López Vigil, "Cuban Women's History," 42.
10 López Vigil, "Cuban Women's History," 43.
11 López Vigil, "Cuban Women's History," 43.
12 Laurie Brand, *Women, the State, and Political Liberalization: Middle Eastern and North African Experiences* (New York: Columbia University Press, 1998), 219.

Vitality in Precarious Conditions

Conversation with Artist/Art Critic Tonel

In November 2002 in Havana, I had the fortune to meet and interview the artist and art critic Antonio Eligio Fernández, or Tonel, as he is known. Tonel is an internationally known Cuban artist, art critic, and curator. His vast oeuvre includes textured ink drawings and cutout wood sculptures. His works are held in the National Museum of Fine Arts in Havana, the Ludwig Forum für Internationale Kunst in Aachen, Germany, and the Lehigh University Art Galleries in Bethlehem, Pennsylvania, among other places. I spoke to him about the Cuban art scene during a period of great vitality and precariousness in the 1990s as artists were entering into the international market and taking new risks with their art. We also spoke about the difference between artists of the 1980s and 1990s and the validity of distinguishing between "generations" of artists as defined by decades.

SUJATHA FERNANDES: Some people have referred to the period from 1989 as a period of silence in the visual arts. What is the situation of the visual arts a decade later?

TONEL: A period of *relative* silence. And what I mean is that, for a while, everything felt very quiet. I remember that I had written an article where I said that I felt the silence in Havana, above all between 1990 and 1993, more or less. It had to do with the fact that my generation—that is, most of the artists who became well known during the 1980s—left Cuba between the late 1980s and the early 1990s. They migrated, and almost all were soon established in Mexico, other Latin American countries, the United States, or Europe. Suddenly it was as though they had cut professional relations, and also personal relationships at the same time, with many of those who had stayed in Cuba. And the silence—I think that has to do also with the idea that all Cuban life had been diminished in so many aspects, extinguished almost in certain ways, descended to a minimal level in the first years of the 1990s, in art as well as in the social, economic, and cultural realms. This is the moment of crisis that was officially termed the special period.

There were some international exhibitions in 1990 and 1991 that summarized the art of the 1980s: Kuba o.k. at the Kunstalle in Dusseldorf and No Man Is an Island, an exhibition that originated in Pori, Finland, and later traveled to Hungary.[1] But there was—for a while, although at times it felt like an eternity—a lull in national life, in the economy, in finance, in production; a lack of electricity and also a lack of energy to do things, the lack of materials to make art and exhibit it. Most venues suffered in this situation, given the precarious state of art centers, galleries, even the National Museum, since it was more difficult than ever before to keep the spaces properly running, to find materials for repairing or maintenance of buildings and infrastructure. And that's without mentioning the difficulties that most artists had to face, in particular to create complex or ambitious installations, or other types of works. This shaped and was reflected in artistic production. And this combination of a generation that is practically abandoning the scene, together with the lack of resources and the stagnation of the country, contributes to a moment that we could refer to as silence.

After this, the Cuban economy begins to readjust and evolve. The legalization of the US dollar in 1993; the 1994 exodus of *balseros*;[2] more Cubans leaving the country as immigrants, who eventually would send dollars to their families on the island; and the steady growth in tourism. All of these factors, among others, led to a relative if slow recovery of the Cuban economy and of social life. It was a recovery from below zero to a place where life could be considered closer to what was normal for people in this country before the 1990s. Now [in 2002] the circumstances are different. The manner of producing art has changed. The market has greater influence in the art scene of today. The focus of many artists has also changed. Earlier (say, during the 1980s and before), artists in this country were very focused on making their mark, leaving a legacy, having an impact on the local Cuban scene. This still happens to a great extent, but it is increasingly perceived as a kind of transition, as a foundation from which to jump beyond the local, given the new possibilities of insertion into international, global circuits. I think that this is changing the role of the local art spaces, of those venues including the Havana Biennial where for quite a while we have had the most important discussions about making, showing, and assessing contemporary Cuban art.

With the new importance of the market, we have the arrival as well of certain expectations and certain desires. People (I am thinking of some of the potential buyers, who are mostly foreigners) may be looking for a painting that goes well with the furniture in their house. Their intentions could be more decorative or focused on art as a commodity, as an object, something that is the result of a traditional craft. These are just some of the elements in the transactions taking place in this Cuban art market, and reality is always more complex, of course. But the taste that the market imposes corresponds to certain notions of what art is and should be, and these notions can often be very conservative. And the trend toward creating and expanding new collections of contemporary Cuban art could end up promoting a type of local artistic production that tries to satisfy a foreign taste in themes, iconography, aesthetic choices to fit this new external aim for collecting.

On top of that, there are new and increasing expectations, especially coming from foreign curators, collectors, and even dealers, regarding the fact that Cuban art should be political, or that it should fulfill expectations of being a sort of "critical art" that refers directly to particular aspects of Cuba's reality. This deserves some further comments. First, from outside the country, there is at times this belief that Cuban intellectual production (in particular before the late 1980s and early 1990s) never had a critical character during the revolutionary period. So, when people think of certain works that were created and became well known or that were the sources of controversy during recent years, they may think that these controversies and frictions are totally exceptional, that they exist in a historical vacuum.

I feel that there is an assumption, sometimes, that critical art or literature or cinema was too scarce or nowhere to be found in Cuban history, before the celebrated art movement of the late 1980s. Or it happens that previous works that could be considered critical, controversial, have not always been acknowledged as much as they deserve. When I say this I have in mind, for instance, certain films by Gutiérrez Alea, Guillén Landrián, or Sara Gómez; zones in the poetry of Virgilio Piñera or Rafael Alcides; and of course artworks by Antonia Eiriz, Chago Armada, even the early Tomás Sánchez, just to mention a few. In terms of works created more recently, off the top of my head I could think of songs coming out of the timba movement and then the hip hop movement during the 1990s, or films by Fernando Pérez, or certain zones in the poetry of Carlos Augusto Alfonso. I could give you an example based on my own experience. I have noticed that when I show images of Cuban art outside of Cuba, in the US or Europe, sometimes people are surprised that certain artworks have been made in Cuba at any given historical time. On the other hand, some of the more controversial or more openly discussed artworks from the recent past (think again of works from the late 1980s, for instance) have been magnified, and this in turn has helped to create a particular or narrow notion of what Cuban art is. It is a perception that has also helped to define Cuban art for the broader public, above all for foreign audiences.

As the growth in demand and the increasing interest of the foreign market become more prominent, there is a growing presence of buyers, collectors, and dealers who come to Cuba looking for a supposedly "well-made" painting or artifact. Also very noticeable has been the presence of buyers who are looking for art with local color, with a particular Cuban flavor: Caribbean, tropical, critical, socialist (or postcommunist) art, that satisfies this kind of demand.

In any case, what I see in Cuba today is vitality in very precarious conditions: a vitality that nonetheless has survived within an important institutional chain that goes from the art schools and national academies to the institutions, spaces, and venues where artists exhibit their works (art centers, commercial galleries, etc.). Historically there has been a hierarchical order to these different venues, the most important being, since its inception in 1984, the Havana Biennial. New elements have been added to this art system, for instance the connection to the international art market and the participation in what we could term "global" institutions, by artists who are sometimes based mostly in Cuba and by other artists who these days spend most of their time abroad. This system is like a machinery of sorts, a machinery that may be damaged and at any moment can stop, can be missing a key part, or that contains parts that are worn out, not in the best shape. There is diversity in the current art scene. This has almost always been a feature of Cuban art. But I also sense that the local atmosphere has turned into something a little provincial, parochial perhaps. The way to go beyond this provincialism, I think, would be reconnecting in a more fluid manner with the world, with external spaces and institutions, with cities, centers, and artists way beyond Havana.

FERNANDES: I know that it's difficult to speak about phases of art, but how can we understand the 1980s and 1990s in Cuba?

TONEL: The 1980s were a very dynamic period in terms of Cuban culture and a phase of renewal for the visual arts. In particular toward the end of that decade, the Cuban art movement captured the attention (the imagination, we could say) of several important art critics, journalists, curators, museum people, artists from all over the world. The Havana Biennial was a key factor in this development. Perhaps it would be useful to go a little further back, in historical terms, toward the end of the 1970s, when there was a gradual but visible expansion of Cuban art in new directions, and some of the artists who became acclaimed and well known during the 1980s started their careers.

From the very end of the 1970s on, artists began to explore paths that they had not traveled before: in themes, media, styles, awareness of then-recent international developments. A connection to the New York art scene was reactivated; the presence of Ana Mendieta in Cuba during the early 1980s is a great example of that. Artists began to travel more frequently abroad, to make contact more often with the universe of art in world centers. So, by the start of the 1980s, Cuban art will be present again in the Venice Biennial, the São Paulo Biennial, the Biennial for Young Artists in Paris. Then Cuba begins to organize its own biennial, which took place for the first time in 1984 in Havana. This event is a prominent sign of a cultural phase that brought Cuban art closer to the art of the so-called Third World. Starting from the late 1970s and all the way through the 1980s, the links with international art and culture became stronger, went beyond the traditional relationship with Latin America or with the nations of the Communist Bloc.

Toward the end of the 1980s there was a general situation of extreme tension between artists and politicians that resulted in some episodes of censorship, which in turn provoked more tension. Artists felt mistreated. Some of the best-known examples of this censorship took place around the Proyecto Castillo de La Fuerza (Castillo de La Fuerza project), which was a series of group shows, held in 1989, featuring the work of the younger generation. Then in 1990, during the opening of El objeto esculturado

(The sculpted object) at the Centro de Desarrollo de las Artes Visuales, a surprise performance by Àngel Delgado was deemed unacceptable and provoked a scandal. The show was canceled, and Delgado ended up spending six months in jail.

But, perhaps paradoxically, I do think that during the 1990s artists had much more space to do things and express themselves, to refer to topics that had been taboo in previous times. For example, the Havana Biennial of May 1994 happened right before the balseros crisis of August of that same year. Several Cuban artists (Kcho, Sandra Ramos, Tania Bruguera, Manuel Piña) dealt with the topic of migrants and boat people in their works for this exhibition, and in a sense they anticipated the national crisis that exploded a few months later. What is important is that artists took up the more-or-less taboo (in the public discourse) topic of the balseros, and by showcasing it in an international event with a great level of visibility they brought it to the mainstream, so to speak, of Cuban culture. Of course, the organizers of the Biennial deserve all the credit as well, for including these works in the event. We can also consider the at-times heavy-handed censorship during the 1980s toward works that dealt with sexuality and eroticism. In the 1990s, artworks took on the topic of sexuality much more openly, and for the most part without facing a harsh institutional backlash.

When we think of the 1990s, we're talking about a new generation of artists and a totally different socioeconomic and cultural situation in the island. If the earlier generation (the artists from the 1980s) had stayed in Cuba, making and promoting their art in their country, I don't know what kind of art they would have produced. We will never know, because many of the most outstanding among them went to Mexico, Spain, Latin America, and finally Miami. The change of context for them couldn't have been starker, and their works often suffered in the new social and cultural environments.

The 1990s brought not just new artists, but also new themes and perspectives. Garaicoa has made art about the Cuban troops in Angola, the "internationalists," from a point of view that was not fully in agreement with the established, official versions about that war, here in Cuba. The same goes for many of the artworks done by Kcho about immigration, or some of the performances and projects by Tania Bruguera. I don't know if the artists who decided to go and stay outside of Cuba would have reacted to their reality in the same way as these young artists who have stayed and worked here. The new artworks by the younger 1990s generation are being exhibited and discussed both in Cuba and abroad. Some of them introduce history, politics, religion, race, and gender issues in ways that, during the 1980s, probably would have invited some sort of censorship. I am thinking of some of the works from the mid-to-late 1990s by Fernando Rodríguez, Pedro Álvarez, Douglas Pérez, Juan Carlos Alom, to mention just a few.

In the 1990s, the institutions, the people with power in the cultural sphere, understood, to a certain degree, that there are artistic works and discourses that have to be left out there, presented for the people to see them, for the audiences to discuss, share, and understand as part of a normal social and cultural process. Those discussions will be for the most part limited to the confines of the exhibition space. The national media, the newspaper *Granma* and other publications with a wide readership, will never print an article about certain works of art that could be deemed too controversial. Overall, comparing the situation of the 1990s with that of the 1980s, I would say that the cultural climate of the last few years has been more relaxed; there has been more flexibility and fewer controversies about themes that could be considered taboo. Artists have introduced new themes and perspectives, and there seems to be more space for maneuvering within the institutions. This doesn't imply that the cultural and artistic spheres constitute a harmonious, peaceful paradise; quite the opposite.

FERNANDES: How would you define conceptual art and commercial art? Is there a dialogue between these two, or do they function in distinct spheres?

TONEL: I don't distinguish between conceptual art and commercial art. With conceptual art you are referring to a particular tendency, let's say a more intellectual art, more concerned in truly questioning reality, seriously interrogating and expressing reality. But that kind of art is sold and bought. There is a market for it; there are galleries promoting it and institutions showcasing it. I think that certain forms of art can seem more oriented toward, or better suited for, specific sections of the art market, and that positioning could be called at times "commercial." In Cuba, these "conceptual" and "commercial" trends coexist. Perhaps you have met or will meet with an artist who moves between both sides. When we say "conceptual" or "commercial," we're not talking about static, immobile definitions, nor are we talking about artists who stay firmly on just one side of the equation. We're talking about things that are complex and can be intertwined, that have evolved, drifting apart or converging.

If you think about the work of Kcho—to mention a well-known and successful young artist—you realize that his is the kind of work that has a serious, intellectual side to it, while it is also accepted in the market, embraced by galleries, institutions, collectors. The label ("conceptual," "commercial," etc.) that is applied to certain works doesn't always depend on the work itself. It could be a by-product of who is promoting the art, exhibiting it; who is trying to sell it, to buy it, to collect it, to give it a prize. I think that there is more often than not an intersection between these two spheres or realms. One is the sphere of an art that is created under serious intellectual and aesthetic premises, that could be considered substantial, illuminating, and that simultaneously succeeds at the level of that other sphere that is the art market, in terms of sales, profits, the intervention of galleries, dealers, auction houses, the big global institutions. Kcho's work has been sold by influential galleries, circulated in first-rate circuits and showcased in some of the great centers of today's global art scene. You could say the same of some of the works by Tania Bruguera. Her output takes shape in a variety of media: installation, video, performance. Her work shows intellectual, ideological, cultural concerns, at times with a sense of urgency, of immediacy. It is a work that is being accepted, promoted in spaces that you could consider "commercial," from galleries to some of the major institutions at the center of international art today, places where the market—in ways that can be more or less visible, more direct or indirect—is one very influential factor.

In Cuba, if we think of "commercial," of what seems more appealing to the art market, we should not forget that there is the influence of a certain kind of taste, one that is highly conditioned by collectors, institutions, buyers who are often based outside of Cuba. There is a tendency around here to think of painting as "commercial" and intrinsically more conservative. But for those—mostly foreign—buyers, what can be appealing goes beyond a specific medium or genre. It could be a sculpture, an installation, a print, a photograph. There is also a more overtly commercial kind of work aiming at the market for tourists, for the kind of visitor you can find walking along Calle Obispo in Old Havana. When you go up and down that street, you can see houses and all kinds of small spaces adapted as galleries, partially functioning as a venue for displaying paintings and handcrafted objects. You can buy a painting there for forty, sixty, or a hundred [US] dollars. In these spaces you will find paintings that respond to the expectations that many tourists have of Cuba: old American cars, portraits of Che Guevara, curvy and sexualized mulatto women, landscapes with palm trees, *guajiros* holding cigars, the picturesque view of Viñales Valley. Sometimes these works aimed at the tourist buyer are connected to the broader local art scene in surprising ways. For instance, you may learn that a student at the Instituto Superior de Arte (ISA), who is doing very serious ("conceptual") work at the academy, is also making relatively simple paintings to be sold on the market at Obispo Street. For the art student, this would be a way to have some sort of income, to get the money needed to survive in Havana. I think that artists are usually capable of understanding the different demands of different markets and of bridging the gap between those not-too-distant spheres. With much cynicism, artists can move back and forth from one camp to another.

FERNANDES: If the movement of public art in the 1980s was characterized by a collective spirit, what is the balance between the collective spirit and individual projection in visual arts of the 1990s?

TONEL: The balance during the 1990s is much more inclined toward individual interest. As always, there exists a collective consciousness, and there are times when artists come together to create, gathering around an idea, an exhibition, a project, or an entity like DUPP or Enema [see "Public Art and Art Collectives in Havana"], which have been pedagogical experiences extended as creative outlets, beyond the school. During the 1990s, the definition of individual success increasingly signifies that the art someone is creating makes more money, is profitable.

FERNANDES: You have said that the emigration of artists from the 1980s generation opened the possibility of an "extraterritorial" art. How has this dynamic affected the cultural life of the island?

TONEL: It affects cultural life in a very imperceptible way, because it is a process that is occurring right now, and there is not much awareness in Cuba about it. What is happening is that these artists emigrate, settle abroad, and—if their new life allows for it—start making a kind of art that is conditioned by the social and cultural circumstances of their new environment. In a way it is Cuban art, because these artists have a certain education, an experience of Cuba that connects them forever with their homeland. In some ways, these artists are following the evolution and the logic of art here, in Havana. I think that this is very interesting.

The art being done by Cuban artists who are now based outside of Cuba needs to be understood as part of Cuban society. It is forming an extension, beyond this country, of Cuban culture. But at the same time it is producing a syncretism, contributing to a process of hybridization with Mexican, Spanish, American culture. Think of a work produced by Los Carpinteros in a studio in San Francisco or Madrid. It is not going to be the same as the work that they have produced here in Havana. The installations that Sandra Ramos creates in situ for a show in Mexico are not the same as the ones she would make here. The cultural, material, even the spiritual environments in all of those places have different features and accents, and that is something that must inform the work. Just at the level of available technology, resources, artistic production, there could be important differences between the works made in Havana and those made elsewhere. Those differences matter and must be taken into account.

How is this affecting Cuban culture? I think it is affecting it, because the artists, intellectuals, writers, filmmakers are like members of a family, are connected between them and also to a common tradition. They share experiences, training, and knowledge. Sometimes like at ISA they may have attended the same courses with the same faculty. So, there is a common history that reinforces, shapes, and reshapes the existing traditions. If you are an artist, an intellectual, you try to see, to identify where you are coming from, what was there when you get to the scene, and also what's coming after you, your descendants so to speak. I think that for many artists who left Cuba, there is a possibility of losing the strength of their connection to what happened before, and for the same reason (because of a physical and spiritual distance) there could be a disconnect to what came afterward. When there is a breaking, an interruption of those continuities and connections, we are talking about serious, even tragic stuff.

FERNANDES: How can we understand the difference between the generations? Is there a difference between the generations of the 1980s and 1990s?

TONEL: I think that defining generations by the chronological beginning or ending of decades, according to calendars, is always tricky. In general, it could work, but the cuts are not always clean and final. For instance, from the 1980s and into the 1990s, there was a group of artists who acted as a bridge between the two decades—Tania Bruguera, José Toirac, Ernesto Leal, Carlos Estévez, Luis Gómez, Pedro Álvarez, and other artists who began working and exhibiting by the end of the 1980s. They were just starting out during the late 1980s, but in reality they became much more visible and began to have a much more important presence from the start of the 1990s and on.

Afterward comes the generation of Fernando Rodríguez, Kcho, Los Carpinteros, Osvaldo Yero, Sandra Ramos, Belkis Ayón, Abel Barroso, Esterio Segura, Carlos Garaicoa, to mention just a few. Segura y Garaicoa cocurated, in 1993, what became a defining exhibition for this generation, Las metáforas del templo.[3] These and other young artists, including a great group of photographers (Juan Carlos Alom, Eduardo Muñoz Ordoqui, Manuel Piña, Marta María Pérez, Kattia García Fayat, René Peña, and some others) kept the momentum going for Cuban art during the 1990s. But at any given time—at least in Cuba—there is a tendency to forget about those artists who were there before and who continued offering their contributions, in their own terms, to the local art scene. I believe in art and culture as a process of continuity, with overlapping generations working simultaneously, and all bringing something to the table. For instance, during the 1990s we should highlight some artists from the 1980s who were extremely active and influential: Lázaro Saavedra, Eduardo Ponjuán, René Francisco Rodríguez, Sandra Ceballos, Ezequiel Suárez, Rocío García. And on top of all of the above, we should not forget that also during the 1990s we have older artists working, exhibiting, teaching, participating in the cultural life of the nation.

I remember a gathering of young artists from the 1990s with Raúl Martínez as a guest figure, and a resulting collaboration, around 1994. Chago Armada was around and still showing his work in the early 1990s. Same with Antonio Vidal, Alfredo Sosabravo, Roberto Fabelo, Nelson Domínguez, Manuel Mendive, Tomás Sánchez, Choco, Flora Fong, Ever Fonseca, César Leal, and others from the so-called 1970s, who were all showing, sometimes teaching as well. So there are these paths, very clearly linking the past and the present, that shouldn't be underestimated—nor should they be overestimated. I remember that the artists of the 1980s thought that they had nothing to do with the generation before them. There was at some point a strong reaction, negating almost completely what had happened in the Cuban art scene of the 1970s. I understand to a certain extent these kinds of reactions; they seem almost unavoidable. They are part of a process of self-reaffirmation. But I prefer to believe that together with the differences and with the arrival of the new, there is a sequence, a lineage, the prevalence of historical trends that should not and cannot be overlooked.

Notes

1 *Kuba o.k.: Aktuelle kunst aus Kuba*, Städtische Kunsthalle Düsseldorf, Germany (1990), in collaboration with Centro de Desarrollo de las Artes Visuales of Havana, curated by Jürgen Harten and Antonio Eligio (Tonel); *No Man Is an Island* (Kuuban nuori taide/Joven arte cubano/Young Cuban Art), Pori Taidemuseo, Finland (1990), also presented at Ernst Museum, Budapest, Hungary, curated by Flavio Garciandía, Marta María Pérez, and Marketta Seppälä.

2 *Balseros* (rafters) is the name given to those Cubans leaving the country for the United States on improvised balsas or rafts, enduring a treacherous journey by sea during which many have lost their lives over the years. In the August 1994 exodus, more than thirty-five thousand Cubans left the country on rafts.

3 *Las metáforas del templo* (The metaphors of the temple), Centro de Desarrollo de las Artes Visuales, Havana, curated by Carlos Garaicoa and Esterio Segura, with participating artists Abel Barroso, Alberto Casado, Los Carpinteros (Alexandre Arrechea, Marco Castillo, Dagoberto Rodríguez), Carlos Garaicoa, Ernesto García, Jorge Luis Marrero, Douglas Pérez, Fernando Rodríguez, Esterio Segura, and Osvaldo Yero.

Public Art and Art Collectives in Havana

In the summer of 1991, residents of Havana noticed the numbers "6" and "39" painted at various locations in the city—on buildings, pylons, and other random places. The numbers provoked much discussion and speculation. People going about their daily routines would pause to look at them. Residents commented on their genesis, and rumors spread about their possible source. The numbers had been painted by the artist Carlos Garaicoa, a pioneer in what would come to be a movement of public art and art collectives during the 1990s. Given the uncertainty of these early days of the special period, rumor was an avenue for self-expression and communication that had no parallels in the official art world.

After the early years of the special period, marked by a shortage of materials, an exodus of artists, and censorship, artists began to reconsolidate under the new conditions imposed by the foreign art market and ongoing censorship of the arts. The late 1990s and early 2000s also saw the reemergence of public art as a movement of visual artists, including art teachers and their students, who sought to revive collective art-making and negotiate with state institutions for inclusion. Arts teachers began to popularize the notion of public art as a way of renovating an ethos of collectivism against the encroachments of the international art market. Unlike more established artists, art students had little opportunity to travel and sell their work to foreign buyers and were more dependent on the state for their subsistence. Students produced art dealing with contentious social and political themes, and they negotiated with the state for the rights to display their critical works.

From Collaboration to Negotiation

The emergence of radical critical art in Cuba is generally identified with the Volumen Uno (Volume one) group, whose exhibition opened on January 14, 1981, in the Centro de Arte International in Havana. This exhibition by such artists as José Bedia, Juan Francisco Elso Padilla, and Flavio Garcandía was the starting point for a series of group shows that represented an important departure from established Cuban art traditions. The exhibition opened the way for self-referential issues within art and began an incursion into the international art world. It also heralded the use of new techniques such as hyperrealism and performance art.

During the 1980s, Cuban visual artists built on the atmosphere of critical activism and the challenging of taboos that accompanied the political climate. One of the main forms they used was public art. Artists carried out "happenings," which varied from carefully staged performances to improvised, spontaneous events. Around 1986, young artists came onto the art scene in collectives, including Grupo Provisional, Arte Calle, Grupo Puré, and Grupo Imán. Seeking to destabilize institutional norms and established procedures, they used irreverence and parody to convey their messages. For instance, during an event held by the Writers and Artists Union (UNEAC) in 1986, two young artists, Consuelo Castañeda and Humberto Castro, burst in wearing giant penis costumes and spraying milk on the panelists.[1] The following year, the members of Grupo Provisional barged into an UNEAC conference on art, turning it into a pompous award ceremony and offering skeletons emblazoned with the word "artist" to the "winners."[2] Artists sought to challenge the conventions of the art world and its methods of bestowing legitimacy.

However, art collectives of the 1980s attempted to go beyond criticism of the art world to address society and politics in general. Art critic Gerardo Mosquera says that in the 1980s, the visual arts "took on the role of assemblies as well as the totally controlled mass media as they converted themselves into a space for expressing the problems of ordinary people." Out of all the art forms, Mosquera says that "the visual arts became the most daring platform, and some street performances... were true demonstrations."[3] The criticisms continued to grow stronger, until a series of events in 1989–90 dispersed the groups. In February 1989, an exhibition at the Castillo de la Real Fuerza was closed when it was found to include a portrait of Fidel Castro, portrayed in drag, with large breasts, and leading a political rally. Marcia Leiseca, the vice minister of culture, was relocated to the Casa de las Américas.[4] In response, artists organized a baseball game at the José A. Echeverría Stadium, where permission is needed for a gathering but not for a ball game. But when the group Paideia read to the crowd a manifesto denouncing the "subordination of the intellectual to hegemonic structure," the stadium was immediately cleared.[5] The confrontation between artists and the authorities came to a head at an exhibition at the Centro de Desarrollo de las Artes Visuales in 1990. After defecating on a copy of the official newspaper *Granma,* Ángel Delgado was declared guilty of public scandal and sentenced to six months in prison.

The series of clashes between artists and the state in the late 1980s and the subsequent exodus of artists changed the way in which the state dealt with artists. During the 1980s, artists had greater access to power, partly due to the influence of Marcia Leiseca, and they worked with the state to devise cultural policy. But as artists became more daring and bold in their cultural expressions, the level of tension increased. Artist Tania Bruguera noted, "In the 1980s they had their feet on our necks. It was a time of *machista* confrontations. Meanwhile, they learned, everyone learned—the artists and those in power." Over the next decade, the level of confrontation and censorship decreased because both artists and the state understood the rules of the new game. As Bruguera said, "If in the 1980s there had been a collaboration with the government to create things, in the 1990s there was an understanding, which is different because it is not the same access to power. It is more passive and submissive."

By the 1990s, repression and economic crisis had severely weakened the visual arts in Cuba. Many artists ceased work for lack of institutional support. It was difficult to find art supplies, and artists had no income. The difficulties of working in Cuba led to mass migrations of Cuban visual artists to the United States, Mexico, and elsewhere in Latin America. Many of them severed personal and professional ties with Cuba as they started over. The combination of a generation that had abandoned the art scene, the lack of resources, the stagnation of the country, and censorship led to a situation that many referred to as a period of silence in the Cuban visual arts.

The Global Art Market

The visual arts were revived after the exodus of the early 1990s largely through the production, distribution, and exhibition of Cuban art in international circuits. Before the 1990s, Cuban artists had few opportunities to exhibit and sell their work abroad because of the US embargo and restrictions imposed by the Cuban government. When intercultural exchange took place in the 1970s and 1980s, it was mostly with the Soviet Union and other countries of Eastern Europe. After the collapse of the Soviet Union, these barriers began to break down. In 1988, the US Congress amended the embargo to allow the exchange of information materials. But this did not include Cuban art. Sandra Levinson from the Center for Cuban Studies was part of a successful lawsuit brought by the National Emergency Civil Liberties Committee against the US Treasury Department and the Office of Foreign Assets Control in 1991. After the lawsuit, the importation and sale of Cuban art was legalized, and artists and curators began traveling back and forth between Cuba and the United States.

As visual artists, musicians, and writers became important financial and symbolic assets to the Cuban state, they were granted various privileges not available to other Cubans. In 1993, the Cuban government passed a resolution to allow artists to receive payment in convertible currency for work they sold abroad. They were able to establish direct relations with international galleries, collectors, and institutions for sale of their artworks and for residencies, tours, and exhibitions. The international exhibition of contemporary art known as the Havana Biennial brought many Cuban artists in contact with foreign curators, artists, and buyers.

Tourism and the international art market encouraged the production of artwork and craft that catered to those markets, and the promotion of individual artists assumed unprecedented importance. A few highly mobile visual artists had access to sums of money that most Cubans could only dream of, making them part of an upper middle class. As more established artists moved up and out of Cuba, visual arts were sustained by those artists who remained working in Cuba. Whereas transnational artists focused on gallery exhibitions, paintings, sculpture, and photography, art students took art into the streets, much as the 1980s generation did. Their emphasis on public art, performance art, and interactive activities played an important role in making the visual arts part of the lives of ordinary Cubans.

The Revival of Public and Collective Art

The increasing hegemony of the art market in Cuba prompted a return to public art in the late 1990s. In 1997, the artist and teacher René Francisco Rodríguez helped to organize the group DUPP among his students at the ISA, including Wilfredo Prieto, Joan Capote, Inti Hernández, and Juan Rivero. Until then, the younger artists had been looking mainly to the international art market with hopes of working abroad. With DUPP, artists turned their attention to the development of cultural life in Havana, reviving the idea of collectives and working in public spaces. In 1999, another group of students from ISA began putting out a magazine. The artist Lázaro Saavedra entered ISA, and with his experience in performance, he helped the students to form the group ENEMA, whose members worked with their bodies in performance. Another group, Departamento de Intervenciones Públicas (Department of Public Performances, DIP), emerged later with the intention of working in the city and in open spaces, away from institutions and galleries. According to Rodríguez, the agenda of groups such as DUPP was to revitalize the political spirit of art in the face of its commercialization. He said, "We propose somehow to rescue the spirit of the 1980s, this transgressive spirit committed to social contexts, committed to the necessity of speaking out and not thinking so much about how I can make my next work so it will sell, but how I can construct my next work so it will communicate with the public. We want to break with this commercial art that is increasingly empty and cold."

The art collectives relied strongly on a notion of self-knowledge and personal exploration. Their interpretation of the collective relied on an understanding of how communities sustained individual growth. Members of art collectives in Havana saw the values of community and individual self-cultivation as contrasting markedly with the ideas of individualism being introduced by the art market. Lino Fernández, a member of ENEMA, emphasized, "Working as a collective challenges the idea of the work as an individual act that is done at a certain time for a certain public. The work of any one of us rejects the idea of the author and challenges the idea of performance as something that can't be repeated."

In 2000, ENEMA decided to curate a show of male transvestites within the ISA. Transvestites have generally been an invisible and marginalized group in Cuban society. Although they acquired a somewhat higher profile in the 1990s, transvestite performers were still excluded from mainstream institutions and venues. The members of ENEMA decided that transvestite performances should be recognized as a valid form of artistic expression, and this was the argument they put to the department heads of ISA. "The main problem we faced," Fernández explained, "was that ISA was an academic institution, and they didn't permit anything they didn't consider arts to be presented in an academic institution. But it was precisely with this in mind that we made this proposal. It was to demonstrate that there were other ways of making art. Many of them had never seen a drag show, so they were judging it without knowing anything about it. We were looking for confrontation and debate." In the end, the show was permitted to go ahead. The encounter with the art school leaders was an important experience for the young artists of ENEMA, who were involved in long meetings with ISA's top directors. The staging of a controversial performance within a state institution was part of the new dynamic of young artists seeking to negotiate with institutions.

Artist collectives sought to defend their work as art rather than politics. The group published several issues of their newspaper, self-titled *ENEMA*, and at the Havana Biennial in 2000 presented their video of a news broadcast called *NOTINEMA*, modeled on Cuba's only television newscast, *Noticieros*. The broadcast presented ENEMA's actions and performances using a mass medium that is a state monopoly. Artist collectives have at times taken on the function of what Rodríguez calls "microministries of culture," becoming institutions for promoting and disseminating art.

Negotiation with the state amplified the scope of what was possible in cultural politics but also helped to delineate the boundaries of what was officially permissible. Two pieces shown at an exhibition by Wilfredo Prieto of DUPP at the state-run Centro de Arte Contemporáneo Wilfredo Lam in 2002 were deemed offensive by the authorities. One piece, *Papel periódico y papel sanitario* (Newsprint and toilet paper), consisted of a roll of toilet paper made out of the newspaper *Granma*. The other was a video of feces moving clockwise around a toilet, titled *Planetas* (Planets). Officials of the Ministry of Culture and the Ministry of Foreign Relations found *Papel periódico* offensive because Fidel Castro's name was on a sheet of newspaper on the toilet-paper roll. Prieto refused to remove either work, saying he would withdraw the entire exhibition if those two were banned. He argued that *Papel periódico* made a statement about the real lives of most Cubans, who have no toilet paper and therefore make do with the pages of *Granma*. After several discussions between high-level bureaucrats and artists intervening on behalf of Prieto, the pieces were allowed to stay. When the minister of culture visited the exhibition later, he praised it as a powerful tribute to the revolution.

Visual artists of the 1990s were preoccupied with the scatological. Prieto's pieces, the name of the group ENEMA, and Delgado's earlier defecation on a copy of *Granma* reflected the growing popularity of the scatological in international art. References to excrement were transgressive of the norms of official cultural circles, which sought to dissociate themselves from the vulgar and the bodily.[6] The frequent association of *Granma* with feces was an attempt to defy the strictures of revolutionary purity and acknowledge bodily processes, marginality, and the impure. The work of Delgado and Prieto drew the ire of officials because it threatened to disrupt the neat categories through which social life was ordered, contained, and policed.

While some groups sought to create space for critical art through negotiation with state institutions, others did not seek permission for their bold acts. The group DIP carried out several performances in public space to highlight questions of power and surveillance. Ruslan Torres, a member of DIP, described DIP's concept of power and its contrast with that of an earlier era: "For the 1980s generation it was very political to use an image of Fidel Castro. We don't talk so much about Castro; we talk about power. We are more interested in the psychological, because when you address the psychological aspects of surveillance, you're talking about politics in a much stronger form than a painting that says, 'Down with surveillance,' as in the 1980s. I think Cuban art never stopped being political. What changed is the form." Its Foucauldian concept of power contributed to DIP's ability to evade censorship. When power is seen as dispersed, it can be confronted in the psychology of individuals, which is harder to police.

One of DIP's actions was to create identity cards inscribed with the group's full name, Departamento de Intervenciones Públicas, to test the way officials control public spaces. The members of the group produced these cards whenever they were stopped by the police, and the cards looked so official that the police let them pass. Presenting the card is both an act of empowerment for young people who are harassed by police on the streets and a means of demonstrating how authority and control operate.

Another public performance—this one exploring how ordinary Cubans responded to official mandates—was planned for July 4, 2002. On that day, Cuban Americans had threatened to send boats to Havana to bring Cubans to Miami, and police were to be posted on the Malecón. Members of DIP sent citations to people whose names they chose at random from the phone directory, ordering them to be at the Malecón at a particular time on July 4. According to Torres, none of the recipients knew why they had been summoned. Suspicion and tension were palpable when a large group arrived at the Malecón in response to the false citations. The action was an indictment of citizens' obedience to official mandates, but it was also a demonstration that state power can easily be usurped.

The artists sought to expose the contradictions experienced by Cubans who were forced to resort to the black market for basic goods and services, due to soaring inflation and a dual peso-dollar economy. In 1999, the artists' collective DUPP organized a public performance in a large department store, La Epoca, in Central Havana. The store was always full of people who came to look at the items and fantasize about owning them, but few Cubans could actually afford the prices. The public performance involved turning the department store into a museum, because, according to Wilfredo Prieto, "in La Epoca everything is sold in dollars, but people don't have dollars, so how do you buy in dollars?" The DUPP members stationed themselves throughout the store, interfering in the process of buying and selling. One made announcements over a speakerphone to promote the various exhibits. Others were strategically placed in the windows as living models. In a textile display, the artists put labels on the fabrics as if they were exhibits in the gallery. Some people had come to see the performance, as DUPP had advertised it all over the city, but many people had come just to see the store's offerings. Prieto claimed that the idea was not to break up the store's commercial activities but rather to make people aware of their absurdity.

Similarly, in 1999, artist Manuel Piña created a series of placards that he called *Labores domésticos* (Domestic labors). On one placard was an image of a hand signaling "stop," and next to it were the words, "Stop! Enough of this stupidity. You can't be such a shit-eater. STEAL!" The placards were part of a catalog for an exhibition to be held in Tirana, Albania, but the exhibition was canceled for lack of funds. They were also supposed to be part of an exhibition in the II Salon de Arte Contemporáneo in Havana, but it too was canceled. Many people were able to see the placards before they were censored because a large group was involved in organizing the Salon exhibition and because the Tirana exhibition catalog circulated widely in Havana. The placards appeared quite aggressive. Piña called them "shock therapy," forcing people to be honest rather than hiding behind false values and ideals that no longer made sense. Stealing may have been undesirable and morally unethical before the special period, but buying goods on the black market that employees had pilfered from department stores came to be the only means of alleviating critical shortages.

During the 1990s, artists sought to promote negotiation and incorporation into cultural institutions. This reflected both a certain level of co-optation by the state and the efforts of some visual artists to rebuild artistic movements within Cuba after the crisis of the special period. Institutions themselves, such as ISA, became sites of cultural contestation, as artists sought to broaden the scope of what was officially seen as art and to amplify the sphere of the politically permissible. In the words of Cuban artist and art critic Lupe Álvarez, "Cultural institutions were not to be 'assisted' nor to be denied, but were to be penetrated in spite of themselves, in order to fulfill our goals, in spite of them."[7] After the confrontations of the 1980s, the state became more sophisticated in its dealings with artists, but artists also adapted their approach and work in order to continue their access to power.

Work in underground spaces and transnational networks during the 1990s gave a critical edge to the visual arts. At the same time, even though younger visual artists were cynical about the art market, they sought ways to leverage it to give themselves a degree of agency. While the artists of the 1980s had more access to government funding for their art, those of the 1990s were forced to become streetwise. Members of ENEMA wanted to make their serious work commercially viable, and they hoped that eventually they could finance it through sales of their video *NOTINEMA* and other projects. Torres noted that young artists knew they were devaluing their own work by selling images of bodegas and Chevrolets in the Plaza, but they accepted such contradictions with great cynicism.

Notes

1 Luis Camnitzer, *New Art of Cuba* (Austin: University of Texas Press, 1993), 177.

2 Camnitzer, *New Art of Cuba*, 179.

3 Gerardo Mosquera, "The Infinite Island: Introduction to New Cuban Art," in *Contemporary Art from Cuba: Irony and Survival on the Utopian Island*, edited by Marilyn A. Zeitlin (New York: Arizona State University Art Museum, 1999), 27.

4 Camnitzer, *New Art of Cuba*, 258.

5 Eugenio Valdés Figueroa, "Solitude Laid Bare in the Garden of the Madhouse," in *Tonel: Lessons of Solitude*, Exhibition Catalog (Vancouver: Canada Council for the Arts, 1996), 17.

6 See, for instance, the work of Peter Stallybrass and Allon White, *The Politics and Poetics of Transgression* (London: Methuen, 1986).

7 Lupe Álvarez, "Accomplice's Probe: Taking the Pulse of 1990s Cuban Art," in *1990s Art from Cuba: A National Residency and Exhibition Program* (New York: Art in General and Longwood Arts Project/Bronx Council on the Arts, 1997).

New Cuban Cinema

Race and Sexuality

The Cuban culture industries underwent significant changes during the special period as a result of their reinsertion into global networks of production, distribution, and consumption. Like the visual arts, the film industry was partly commercialized as a way of enticing foreign investment into Cuba. Through joint film productions with overseas companies, the Cuban government was able to attract badly needed revenue. But at the same time, the entrance of the Cuban culture industries into global markets of entertainment and consumption opened up the site of culture to new contradictions.

Transnational capital has produced a new "politics of difference" that reifies the exotic features of non-Western cultures for market consumption while providing the basis for the emergence of new kinds of identities.[1] For instance, Afro-Cuban themes, previously marginalized in cultural discourse, became more visible in Cuban film as a result of the global market's appetite for Afro-Cuban culture. Discussions about homosexuality and treatment of the topic of race in Cuban cinema of the 1990s were attempts to bolster ever-present critiques and new concerns amid the contradictions of Cuba's insertion into regimes of global capital.

Film Production and the Global Marketplace

Before the onset of the special period, Cuban cinema, like many other national cinemas in Latin America, was nationalized and subsidized by the state. State patronage was part of a project of national cultural renewal. The Cuban cinema industry was nationalized in 1961, with the creation of the Cuban Film Institute (ICAIC). All film production in ICAIC was directed by a central administrative body. Processes of centralization in the Cuban economy during the 1970s led to the further subordination of ICAIC to the state cultural apparatus through incorporation into the Ministry of Culture.[2] These changes were designed to give the ministry greater control over cinema production. In 1981, under decentralization measures, ICAIC was transformed into the Vice Ministry of Film under the Ministry of Culture.

By the middle of the 1980s, film production in Cuba and in other nations was affected by economic crisis, the growing dominance of Hollywood, and the advent of cable television and video, which competed with movies as forms of mass entertainment.[3] Problems in the film industry were initially addressed through restructuring of ICAIC that gave *grupos de creación* (creation groups) greater control over content and production. Three groups, each directed by a filmmaker, oversaw the entire process of scriptwriting and production. However, with the onset of the special period and a financial recession in the film industry, the creation groups were terminated, and the Cuban film industry moved to become self-financing.

During the 1990s, the costs of film production increased while inputs drastically declined. Although Cuban cinema still had large national audiences, expenses could not be covered by box-office receipts, as the cost of a ticket for a regular feature film remained constant at three pesos, or fifteen US cents, despite marked inflation. The film institute sought other ways to generate financing, including coproductions with foreign agencies and distribution abroad. While ICAIC had formerly produced about ten feature films and about fifty short features every year, after the onset of the special period it was able to make only one or two feature films a year with sponsorship from foreign countries, mainly Mexico, Spain, Venezuela, Peru, and Nicaragua.

Joining the global marketplace resuscitated the Cuban film industry somewhat. Filmmakers found that they needed to cater to the demands of international markets in order to secure coproductions and global distribution, and the imperatives of the market produced new trends in Cuban cinema. Themes of sexuality and Afro-Cuban spirituality were seen as particularly appealing to international audiences, given the attractiveness of exoticized difference as a marketable commodity. As the Afro-Cuban actor Luis Alberto García said, "Afro-Cuban religion has been converted into a trope necessary to attract tourists, make money from tourists, and sell the superficial image of Cuba."

Race and Sexuality in Film

For the first three decades of the Cuban Revolution, themes of sexuality and race were mostly absent from Cuban cinema. Representations of homosexuality were present in a few novels, poems, and popular songs. But the 1984 film *Conducta impropia* (Improper conduct), one of the few films to tackle issues of homophobia in Cuba, was made outside of the country. During the 1990s, representations of homosexuality and transvestism became much more open and public in Cuban literature and arts.[4] Cuban film productions in the 1990s included the landmark film *Fresa y chocolate* and the documentary *Mariposas en el andamio* (Butterflies on the scaffold), which focused on transvestites in the town of La Güinera.

Topics related to race were also uncommon in pre-1990s Cuban cinema. With the untimely death of black filmmaker Sara Gómez, before her 1974 film *De cierta manera* (One way or another) was finished, the Cuban film industry lost an important Afro-Cuban voice. Other black filmmakers, such as Sergio Giral, had difficulty making films and having them screened. Giral's 1974 film *El otro Francisco* (The other Francisco) was more acceptable because it dealt with issues of race in the historical context of slavery. But his 1991 film *María Antonia* was highly controversial for its open portrayal of Afro-Cuban religion and sexuality. Giral's other film dealing with contemporary issues, *Techo de vidrio*, was banned because its indictment of administrative corruption was not resolved by a positive critical vision.

Even in the 1990s, as themes of race were dealt with more openly in Cuban cinema, black actors had difficulty finding roles, since the leads were almost always given to white actors. The only black Cuban in *Fresa y chocolate* has no lines to say. Despite the growing marketability of Afro-Cuban themes, black actors and filmmakers are still a minor presence in Cuban film, and it is often white filmmakers such as Fernando Pérez (*La vida es silbar*) and Humberto Solás (*Miel para Oshún*) who write scripts about Afro-Cuban culture and religion.

The career of Gloria Rolando expresses some of the difficulties faced by Afro-Cubans in ICAIC. Since the mid-1970s, Rolando has been producing documentaries with such famous Cuban filmmakers as Santiago Álvarez. But she worked in the film industry for nearly twenty years before she was able to produce her own feature-length film, *Oggun: An Eternal Presence* (1992), with the support of a foreign video company. As Rolando notes, the film "was produced to sell in tourist places and, from 1991 to this year 1996, it has never been seen on Cuban television."[5] After that, Rolando chose to work independently with Imágenes del Caribe, the video company that she started herself.

Films of the Special Period: **Fresa y chocolate *and* La vida es silbar**

One of the initial attempts by filmmakers to tackle issues of sexuality in the post-Soviet period was the film *Fresa y chocolate* (Strawberry and chocolate), directed by Tomás Gutiérrez Alea in 1994. The film is about the relationship between David, a young orthodox Marxist of working-class background, and Diego, a gay man with upper-class sensibilities, who strikes up a conversation with David one day at the famous ice-cream parlor Coppelia. David, suspicious of Diego's revolutionary credentials and feeling threatened by his advances, reports him to Miguel, the leader of the Union of Communist Youth (UJC), who then orders David to establish a friendship with Diego in order to keep an eye on his activities. The film follows the developing relationship between the two as David is forced to confront his views not only of homosexuality but also of the rigidity of the revolution's Marxist orthodoxy and his own entrapment in it. Diego represents a complex of values: Cuban culture and tradition, bourgeois extravagance, and prerevolutionary nostalgia. The figure of the homosexual in the film functions as the repository of primordial notions of national culture to which Cubans must return.

Critics analyzed *Fresa y chocolate* as an allegory of political reconciliation orchestrated by the state, given the revolution's repression of gay men. They argue that the issues are contained within a heterosexual narrative of male friendship that obscures other possible solutions, such as a sexual relationship between men. It is their common love of the nation that allows Diego and David to build a friendship and that facilitates the ethical and political conversion that Diego brings about in David.[6] But critics suggest that this narrative is stage-managed to avoid modification of nationality or heterosexual masculinity.[7] Subversive aspects of the dialogue are manipulated to repress the ambiguities of the relationship between homosexuals and the state. Both the Davids and the Diegos, the fervent party militants and the disillusioned socialists, must work toward a new revolutionary utopia based on inclusion, tolerance, and friendship.

At the same time, my conversations with Cubans suggest that many supported the filmmakers' attempts to rearticulate the revolution on a more inclusive basis. The fact that the film was banned from Cuban television resists the idea that it was simply a mouthpiece for state policies of reconciliation. It was partly the international and regional successes of the film that created some openings for its ideas within Cuban society. Cuban viewers whom I spoke with reported modifying their deeply held views about sexuality and nationality, often presenting alternative readings of the film. Some viewers said that the film showed how Cubans have operated with a Manichean division of the world into revolutionaries and counterrevolutionaries, with the latter encompassing not only those who oppose the Cuban government, but those who have alternative ideas, visions, philosophies, and marginalized identities. They argued that the family sentiment and humanity they saw embodied in the figure of Diego should be valued, rather than the macho concept of *hombría* (manliness).

While several Cuban viewers saw the film as inaugurating a period of tolerance in Cuban society, they thought that it did not go far enough in dealing with the problems raised. According to the film, gay men can find their place in Cuban society by participating in the revolution, but not by organizing independently. The Cuban minister of culture, Abel Prieto, indicated to me, "*Fresa y chocolate* is an artistic synthesis of the kind of unity in diversity that we need. That is to say, Cuban homosexuals have to submit themselves to this process of unity without losing their identity." Despite its critical nature, the film can be tolerated and even promoted by key officials such as the minister of culture because it puts forward a narrative of incorporation rather than autonomy as the basis for recognition. The film obscures rather than transcends those aspects that cannot be contained within its utopian proposition, such as the possibility of independent organizing among LGBTQ people in Cuba.

While *Fresa y chocolate* proposes a reconciliation between the state and gay men, in the 1998 film *La vida es silbar* (Life is to whistle), filmmaker Fernando Pérez focuses on another marginalized sector of society, Afro-Cubans. In this film, the relationship between Cubans and the state is represented by a woman called Cuba and her son, Elpidio. Cuba is becoming estranged from her son because of her constant demands for perfection, and reconciliation between the two must be based on recognition by the mother/state that her sons/citizens are imperfect human beings who have the right to seek personal happiness and individual satisfaction. Pérez criticizes the kind of voluntarism that requires citizens to sacrifice all of their personal needs and desires for the achievement of a single national goal. As the gay man in *Fresa y chocolate* is a signifier of national culture and tradition, so the mother in *La vida es silbar* is a symbol of the regeneration of the national spirit. The nation's recovery depends on a new form of matriarchy, where women are crucial to the reproduction of new revolutionary citizens.

Elpidio Valdés is a young musician from a marginalized background who makes his living by selling fish to tourists. He is a comic-book character, a quintessential hero like Asterix, who is also an anticolonial symbol for many Cubans. Pérez described Elpidio to me as the character who is most rooted in his reality: "Elpidio is the survivor. He fishes on the Malecón. He is the popular figure who lives in the *solar* [tenements], who participates in Afro-Cuban religion." The film opens with Elpidio as a young boy dancing in the classroom to the music of Bola de Nieve. Throughout the film, Elpidio is identified with Afro-Cuban music and the legends of this musical expression, Benny Moré and Bola de Nieve. Elpidio's mother, Cuba, is a large woman who cradles her children in her arms, but her face is always hidden. Cuba is represented as a "mulatta woman," a symbol of Cuban nation-building. The film revives this construction at a time when the nation is being figuratively reborn, while obscuring her face/identity limits the potential of her dangerous sexuality.

The actor who plays Elpidio, Luis Alberto García, suggested to me that the relationship between Elpidio Valdés and Cuba is represented as difficult. Cuba is always trying to control and discipline Elpidio and will not accept him as he is. At the beginning of the film, Elpidio's sister Bebé is shown whistling in class, and she is reprimanded by the teacher. Later, as Elpidio and Bebé are dancing in the classroom, a voice-over is heard: "No, Cuba, this girl won't change. She won't change here. She can't be kept with the others. She has to follow rules." Several other voices are heard, overlapping: "We're not changing our standards." "From a pedagogical point of view, it is incorrect to. . . ." "She has to be like the others. She has to speak, not whistle." The voices represent the disciplinary authority of the state. Bebé, as narrator, says that Cuba loves Elpidio very much but that Elpidio has not turned out the way Cuba wanted, and that is why Cuba has abandoned him.

Despite Cuba's rejection, Elpidio keeps a framed photo of her by his bed, and next to it an image of the Catholic saint Santa Bárbara. Throughout the film, Elpidio converses with, chides, and appeals to Santa Bárbara. The image of the saint is a representation of Elpidio's communication with his mother, Cuba. In the Afro-Cuban religion of Santería, also known as Regla de Ocho or Lucumí, Santa Bárbara is associated with the *oricha* Changó, the oricha of war, struggle, fire, and passion, with whom many Cubans feel a close relationship. Whereas the traditional image of Santa Bárbara is a young girl in a white gown and crown, Pérez shows her as a highly stylized, larger-than-life statue, based on a painting by the Cuban painter Zaida del Río. Her face is a white plaster mask, large red feathers sprout from a straw crown on her head, and her cape is made of red gauze adorned with streamers (red and white are the colors of Changó).

In her right hand she holds a golden goblet, a symbol of Changó's cauldron, and in her left hand she holds a sword, which is identified with Changó's ax. The use of a syncretic image of Saint Bárbara as a mediating object between Elpidio and his mother is part of an overall cinematic strategy to renew Afro-Cuban culture as the basis for national belonging.

As Elpidio becomes more estranged from his mother, he starts a relationship with Chrissy, a foreigner working for Greenpeace, who arrives in Cuba in a hot-air balloon. The conflict between Elpidio and Cuba leads him to become more involved with Chrissy. When Chrissy asks Elpidio to leave with her, he must choose between his personal desires and his commitment to the nation. This dilemma is reflected in the parallel narratives of two other characters in the film. Julia is a middle-aged care provider for senior citizens who has devoted herself entirely to a career and finds herself with a strange affliction: she cannot stop yawning. Mariana is a young dancer in the National Ballet who believes that if she is going to fulfill her dream of dancing the title role in *Giselle*, she must overcome her passion for men, which means denying herself any form of sexual intimacy. Just as Julia has not danced or made love or allowed herself to experience happiness, Mariana has denied herself sexual intimacy for the sake of achieving her goal. In *La vida es silbar*, Pérez explores the personal and psychological costs of extreme single-mindedness, alluding to historical strategies of the socialist state.

Elpidio feels compelled to leave his mother, Cuba, whom he feels is unresponsive to his needs and refuses to listen to him. He speaks to the image of Santa Bárbara: "I'm going to leave you now. If you don't give me a sign, I'm going to cast you away from me, Cuba. I'm leaving with Chrissy." Yet through his relationship with Chrissy, Elpidio ultimately realizes that freedom is within himself and that he can resolve his problems with his mother without leaving the country. It is through his music, the driving, rhythmic, and primal force of the drums, that he can now reconnect with Cuba.

In one of the final scenes, Elpidio addresses Santa Bárbara: "All right. I'll go find you, Mother. I can forget your forgetfulness, your wish to make me so unbelievably perfect. Nobody's perfect. Nobody. Shit! Let me be and think the way I want. No one rules us here." He points to his head. "You taught me that yourself. And now I'm not going to change. I'm not going to change. But I can't live without you, Cuba. I can't. If you can and want, accept me as I am. Make my music take me to you." The threat of exile functions for Elpidio as a way of strengthening his voice. It has given him his mother's attention, and she must now allow him the freedom to think and must accept him for who he is, rather than trying to make him into a "new man." But Pérez suggests that even though Cuba accuses Elpidio of failing to become the new man, his consciousness has changed. He steals some of Chrissy's money, but he returns her wallet. Elpidio cannot live without Cuba. He is not complete without the nation and therefore cannot leave. Throughout this process of reconciliation, Cuba does not appear as a character in her own right. She must be represented. Bonding between Cuba's sons takes place upon the body of the "mulatta,"[8] who is both central to the discourse of national unity and invisible within it.

At the end of the film, all three characters meet in the Plaza de la Revolución, a crucial historic and political site where many of the important events of the revolution took place, and they begin to whistle. The whistle, for Pérez, is a reaffirmation of the individual and the need to seek one's personal happiness. Elpidio is the embodiment of the nation that has become reconciled with the state, and as a marginal young man in society, he can relate to Cuba as a country that has been forced to struggle for its sovereign place in the world. Being Cuban is identified with street culture, with the roots of Santería and rumba, which have been reincorporated into the national imaginary.

The presence of themes such as race and homosexuality in Cuban film of the 1990s generated spaces for public debate and critical discussion. The new market conditions of production in the Cuban film industry gave rise to these openings, but the topics still met resistance within cultural institutions. Films such as *Fresa y chocolate* and *La vida es silbar,* dealing with marginalized sectors of Cuban society such as gay men and Afro-Cubans, sought to reconcile citizens and the state under the rubric of a more inclusive and pluralistic nation, suggesting that despite their differences, Cubans could be unified in their patriotism. But in the global order reconfigured by new kinds of transnational flows, this singular, coherent notion of national identity comes under scrutiny. Some within Cuba, such as hip hop musicians and Afro-Cuban visual artists, appropriated the openings presented by the growing commercial interests in black culture to criticize nationalist discourse, specifically as it excluded black people and erased cultural difference.

Notes

1 Lisa Lowe and David Lloyd, "Introduction," in *The Politics of Culture in the Shadow of Capital*, eds. Lisa Lowe and David Lloyd (Durham, NC: Duke University Press, 1997).
2 Julianne Burton, "Film and Revolution in Cuba: The First Twenty-five Years," in *New Latin American Cinema*, ed. Michael Martin (Detroit: Wayne State University Press), 133–34.
3 Deborah Shaw, *Contemporary Cinema of Latin America: Ten Key Films* (New York: Continuum Press, 2003).
4 Emilio Bejel, *Gay Cuban Nation* (Chicago: University of Chicago Press, 2001).
5 Gloria Rolando, "Africa, the Caribbean, and Afro-America in Cuban Film," in *Afro-Cuban Voices: On Race and Identity in Contemporary Cuba*, eds. Pedro Pérez Sarduy and Jean Stubbs (Gainesville: University Press of Florida, 2000), 132.
6 Bejel, *Gay Cuban Nation*, 158.
7 Paul Julian Smith, "*Fresa y chocolate* (Strawberry and chocolate): Cinema as Guided Tour," in *Vision Machines: Cinema, Literature and Sexuality in Spain and Cuba, 1983–93* (New York: Verso), 81–100.
8 Carollee Bengelsdorf, "(Re)Considering Cuban Women in a Time of Troubles," in *Daughters of the Caliban: Caribbean Women in the Twentieth Century*, ed. Consuelo López Springfield (Bloomington: Indiana University Press, 1997), 245.

The Capital of Rap

Hip Hop Culture in Alamar

This is dedicated to the 'hood
All of East Havana
Calle Concha, La Pachanga
Micro 10, Guiteras
The capital of rap forever.

HERMANOS DE CAUSA, "ANDO COMO ANDO"

About six miles east of Havana, just beyond the aquamarine blue of the Caribbean Sea and the low-density shrubs of the flat plains, stand the tall rectangular buildings of the Alamar housing projects. The cement constructions are covered in chalky white paint that is peeling and has been eaten away in patches by the salty ocean air. Some individual blocks are painted in pink, murky green, or faded red. Here and there is a palm tree or a children's swing set. Apartments are connected by sets of diagonal stairways that begin at ground level. The design is angular and solid. It is no-frills, functional, proletarian housing. On the tops of the buildings, spidery homemade antennas reach for the sky.

The five- and six-story buildings were designed by Soviet architects and constructed by microbrigades, or ordinary people organized into work teams, as a solution to housing shortages in Havana in the 1970s. Slum clearance programs relocated black communities to Alamar from shantytowns such as Llega y Pon, Las Yaguas, and Palo Cagao. The 1970s were a grim era of Cuban history, known euphemistically as the *quinquenio gris* (gray five years, which actually lasted closer to fifteen years), when the orthodoxy of Soviet socialism overshadowed cultural and social life on the island. The heavy and somber buildings, nicknamed "Siberia" by their residents, immortalized the essence of those years. With a population of 300,000 in more than two thousand buildings, Alamar is the largest housing project on the planet. Each prefabricated building bears a stenciled number—D 42, Zona 2—the impersonal stamp of the assembly line.

If Havana was hard hit by the crisis of the special period, Alamar was affected even more. The gasoline shortages meant transportation into the city was less frequently available, and there were longer waits, making it difficult for people to get to work. No tourists were around to hustle dollars from. And the contained nature of the apartments made it harder for residents to start up small businesses like the bodegas cropping up around Central Havana, where entrepreneurs sold ice cream, pastries, or pizza from the front windows of their homes. There were frequent blackouts, water problems, and shortages of cooking gas. And for the young people of the projects, there was nothing to do. It's no wonder that Alamar, often compared with the South Bronx, has been seen as the capital of rap in Cuba.

It was here, to Alamar, that American rappers were brought by the Black August Hip Hop Project to perform before large crowds of Cuban youth at the annual state-sponsored hip hop festival. Black August was established during the 1970s in the California prison system to link resistance movements across the Americas, and the hip hop collective sought to draw connections between radical black activism and hip hop culture. At the 2001 festival in Alamar, I met Julio Cardenas, also known as El Hip-Hop Kid. A tall guy with a short Afro and an earnest expression, Julio was raised by his mother in the neighboring sector of Guanabacoa. As a kid he would rush home from school to watch the B-boys *retandose* and *retarse*—battling—and *tirando cartones*, laying out the cardboard strip, on the back patio of his building. He and his friends watched *Beat Street*, *Fast Forward*, and *Breakin'* and copied the moves. Julio moved to Alamar when he was fifteen and became caught up in the hip hop movement that was taking the community by storm. He went to *moños*, or block parties, where people rapped and DJed.

After finishing school, Julio went on to technical college and completed a degree in civil construction. But he graduated at the height of the special period, when there were no jobs in his field, so he went to work with his grandfather in a nearby fishery, both to earn cash to help his mother and to get the local authorities off his back. Eventually, he found a job as a bridge operator, raising and lowering the bridge that connected Alamar and Cojimar to allow the ships to pass through. The job was a no-brainer: at 7:00 a.m., he would raise the bridge, and by early afternoon, when all the boats had gone through, he would sit back with his friends and exchange news about who had the latest rap magazine from the States and whether they'd heard a particular song from The Pharcyde or EPMD.

In 1996, Julio formed the group Raperos Crazy de Alamar (RCA) with Carlito "Melito," a carpenter, and Yoan. They started out just to amuse themselves, without ambitions of being serious artists. "That moment we were living was so critical, so boring," related Julio. "Everything was closed off and censored. We, the youth, were doing hip hop just to do something, looking for a way of having fun."

Hip hop was a way out of the boredom of low-paying, menial jobs and truncated opportunities. The rap scholar Tricia Rose identified this need to break the cycle of boredom and alienation as one of the factors underlying the rise of hip hop in its birthplace, the Bronx.[1] While Cuba presented quite specific conditions of economic crisis, combined with political restrictions, I realized that this void wasn't peculiar to Cuba. And hip hop wasn't just a distraction from the void: it was a way of re-creating a sense of community and finding spaces of pleasure in the face of atomization, isolation, and the regimentation of life.

Julio and his friends listened to American rap, but they didn't understand the lyrics, and they had no clue how to write their own songs. One day Julio was at the house of the rap producer Pablo Herrera, listening to his latest CDs. He heard the song "Boricuas on Da Set" by Fat Joe, featured on a compilation album. It was a turning point in his life. "'Coñyyyyoooo, ta buena,' I said when I heard it," Julio related. "It was a moment that touched my heart and opened my mind. I was hearing a lot of music from Miami radio, LL Cool J, 2 Live Crew, Queen Latifah, Monie Love, but that song inspired me. I thought it could really be the Latino-American-Cuban connection."

Pablo copied Fat Joe's song onto a cassette, and Julio listened to the poor-quality recording on his beat-up Walkman over and over, every day. "I liked the beat, but I didn't know what to do," said Julio. "I didn't know anything about flow, cadence, rhythm. I'd never studied music. Wow! How am I gonna do it? At the start, it was all a joke. But every day I began to think about a vision of how I wanted to do the song. What was guiding me was the sound of the voices, the mixture of each, and the cadences. I started to rap over the top of this song, write my first lyrics. So when Fat Joe said, 'Oh Boricuas, clap your hands,' I started saying, 'Todo el mundo con los manos arriba, negros, mulatos, blancos.' That was the basis of my first rap, 'Hip hop es mi cultura.' It was an old-school rap, but it reached the people."

Later that year, RCA tried out at the hip hop festival auditions. The musicians faced a panel of three judges—a professor of visual arts, a professor of drama, and a poet who said that their lyrics were undeveloped, lacking in content, and violent. Julio was incensed. "*Asere*, you don't know shit about rap," he thought. "You've never listened to rap in your life! How you gonna sit there and tell me what is rap?"

But by 1999 RCA had not only passed the auditions—they were the stars of a festival that included the famous American artists Mos Def, Talib Kweli, DJ Hi-Tek, dead prez, and Common. The encounter was anticipated with much emotion and excitement by the Cubans. When dead prez rapped, "I'm an African, I'm an African," in front of a crowd of thousands at the festival, the amphitheater resounded with the thundering sound of the Cuban audience chanting back the words. It was Pan-Africanism in motion. But the politics didn't always translate. Unaware of the implications of what he was about to do, the emcee M-1 pulled out a dollar bill on stage and began to burn it with a cigarette lighter, an act considered illegal and a defacement of property in the United States.

"Because of this dollar, the children in my country are dying for crack or for drugs or for bling-bling," he said. The audience went wild. How could he burn a precious dollar bill? "Oye, no, gimme that dollar! I can buy some bread, or some french fries," people in the audience cried. Then he began to burn a ten-dollar bill. "Nooooo! Stop!" screamed the audience. "What is that crazy fucker doing? I could feed my whole family for a month with that." One member of the American delegation, Raquel Rivera, tried translating, explaining to the baffled audience that in America, black people are dying because of the dollar bill. "But here in Cuba," shouted one person, half-seriously, "people are dying of hunger."

Then, inexplicably, during the performance of the pioneer American rapper Mos Def, people started leaving the stadium. "Reyes de la Calle are better than Mos Def," said some kids on their way out. "We can't understand anything he says."

The Latino-American-Cuban connection was somewhat tenuous when subjected to the very real differences of language, culture, and history. To begin with, Alamar was not the South Bronx. Black Cuban youth had good access to higher education—for example, Julio had finished his degree in civil construction—

even if that education didn't necessarily lead to jobs. They did not live in communities ravaged by crack or other drugs, and "bling" was a remote concept.

Second, the black militancy of the American rappers was not comparable to the racial consciousness of Cuban rappers. Black Cuban identity—always expressed within the boundaries of an anticolonial nationalism—was not equivalent to American blackness, shaped through the fiery battles over slavery, desegregation, and civil rights. Cubans didn't have a civil rights movement that brought a discussion of race out into the open. The black-white dichotomy of American race relations did not exist in Cuba. While in much of North America even "one drop" of black blood socially categorized a person as black, Cubans had a much broader spectrum of racial classifications—from the darker-skinned *prietos*, *morenos*, and *negros* to the mixed-race *pardos* and *mulatos*. The militant stance of American rappers, particularly their language of racial justice, appealed to the Cubans. But the categories of American racial politics established by Jim Crow laws in the early twentieth century could not be superimposed on a culture in which racial identity was not so clearly spelled out.

As the century drew to a close, American rap was no longer the epicenter of hip hop for Cubans. Cuban rap was starting to take on its own voice, to develop its own stars and pioneers. When it closed the 1999 festival, RCA received as much applause as, if not more than, the American artists. "This was a defining moment for us as a movement," recalled Julio. "Despite the fact that they were rappers from the US, from the mecca of the world—New York—they weren't better than us. We were rapping and expressing our own realities to our own people."

The annual hip hop festival in Alamar was started in June 1995 by an association of rappers known as Grupo Uno. They worked on a shoestring budget to make the concerts happen, sometimes without electricity, dependent on an ailing sound system or resources donated by friends and neighbors. By the 1999 festival, state institutions had become more involved, providing a professional sound system, transportation to and from the events, and even food for rehearsals. After the 2000 festival, the state disbanded Grupo Uno and entrusted the government-affiliated Youth League with organizing the events. The absorption of hip hop into the state was underway.

At the same time, the state itself was evolving in response to pressures from citizens. The appointment of the long-haired poet Abel Prieto as minister of culture was a reflection of the changes taking place in the cultural sphere. In July 2001, Prieto met with rappers to talk about forming a rap agency. Afterward he pledged his support to Cuban rap as a movement that profoundly reflects "the theme of racial discrimination" and "highlights the dramas of marginalized barrios." It was the first time an official had talked publicly about race and marginality, and with this newfound legitimacy, rappers began to play a greater role in organizing their festival. Rather than having professors sitting as judges on the panels, by the 2001 festival it was the rappers themselves who were adjudicating.

From the beginning, the annual festival was held at the amphitheater in Alamar, a large, open-air stadium with rows of concrete blocks for seating as well as areas of grass. On the opening night in August 2001, the space was filled to capacity, with a sea of young people in baseball caps, bandannas, baseball jerseys, berets, guayaberas, and checkered shirts. The stage was bathed in alternating red and blue flashes from a strobe light. A set of turntables was mounted on a plank of wood held up by giant steel drums. At the front of the stage, speakers towered over the audience. Draped behind the stage was a large Cuban flag, the red triangle with a five-pointed white star visible above the pumping fists of the performers on stage. To the left of the flag was a graffiti piece that read ALAMAR in block letters at the top.

The ugly cement construction of the amphitheater, typical of the surrounding housing projects, came to life with the resounding thrum of the bass, the energy of the crowd with its hands in the air, and the tags of graffiti covering the walls.

At the closing event, the group Reyes de la Calle performed a song about the *balseros*, the Cubans who leave for Miami in boats. The rappers had wanted to include images of the balseros on a screen behind them, but the idea was not acceptable to the president of the Youth League. He told the DJ and hip hop promoter Ariel Fernández, "CNN may be filming it, and this would lend support to the counterrevolutionaries." So Fernández asked Reyes de la Calle to perform the song without the images. The Cuban government could support the rap festival so long as rappers stayed within certain prescribed boundaries, yet some rappers increasingly wanted to talk about more controversial themes. How long would they accept directives from the Youth League president? Censorship was not always the most workable strategy. In these circumstances, there was nothing like a crisis from the North to unite Cubans and give new fire to the meaning of "revolution."

On September 11, 2001, I sat before the television, watching the grainy images of the World Trade Center towers imploding over and over again. I was unsure if this was yet another Hollywood disaster movie or if it had really happened. Fidel was involved in the inauguration of a new school that evening, and his address before a packed hall of elementary school kids was broadcast live on television. He was resplendent in his military fatigues, and for three hours he cajoled, provoked, and meditated on the events of the day before a group of ten- and eleven-year-olds.

"Whenever there is a tragedy like this one, no matter how difficult to avoid it may be, I see no other way but to keep calm," advised Fidel. "And if at some point I am allowed to make a suggestion to an adversary who has been tough with us for many years, we would advise the leaders of the powerful empire to keep their composure, to act calmly, not to be carried away by a fit of rage or hatred and not to start hunting people down, dropping bombs just anywhere."

The Casa de la Cultura at Carlos Tercera and Castillejo in Central Havana was an old mansion that had been converted into a culture center. In the back was an open area where the Youth League had mounted a stage, set up with antiquated speakers and clunky microphone stands. Young people were milling around, waiting through numerous sound checks. Rappers responded with a combination of good humor and resignation to numerous nonfunctioning microphones. They winced at the piercing feedback that assaulted them from speakers placed too close together on the small stage.

This was July 2002, and I was back in Cuba. In the short space of ten months, much had changed. Julio was one of the first of several rappers to leave Cuba—he had stayed on in New York after participating in the first US tour of Cuban rappers. He was sleeping in a room the size of a closet during a bitter New York winter and wondered whether he had made the right decision. He was neither an athlete nor a professional musician with a future in the US or even family in the States to look out for him. He was poor and black, one of the stars of a movement that came up from nothing. To survive in New York, he would have to put his music career on hold and bus tables like many other migrants in the city.

The world had also changed irrevocably. Immediately after the 9/11 attacks, all US airspace was closed to passenger planes leaving Cuba. Canada-bound planes with tourists who had been in Cuba were forced to fly an extra nine hours along the US coast in a harbinger of what was to follow. The United States declared a global war on terror, and the charges of Cuba as a terrorist nation resurfaced, with accusations that the island was harboring fugitives, selling biotechnology, and trading with the enemies of the US. Five Cuban nationals carrying out counterterrorism work in the United States were convicted in a federal court in Miami and sentenced to prison. There were stepped-up efforts by US officials to find and prosecute former Black Panthers in Cuba. Assata Shakur, who had been given political asylum in Cuba following her escape from jail in 1979, would soon be classified by the FBI as a "domestic terrorist" with a bounty of $1 million on her head. Meanwhile, Cuban rappers were organizing events and had become bolder about saying things in public that earlier they had uttered only privately.

At the Casa de la Cultura, the rapper Yosmel, his hair in short dreadlocks, stood before a microphone. Yosmel had changed his name to Sekou Umoja to emphasize his spiritual connections with Africa. He spoke passionately to the gathered crowd: "You have people saying, 'You're Cuban, you're Cuban, but they're not, they're not.' Well, then, where did 'they' come from? They come from Africa. We have Afro-Cubans in Cuba, Afro-Americans in America, Afro-British in England, and if you're born in Russia with this color skin, are you gonna come to Cuba and try to say that I'm Russian?" He paused. There were laughs from the audience; the irony of that last comparison was not lost on them. "You're separating yourself from who you are," he continued. "This is who you are. When someone feels marginalized, it's never because they wanted to feel that way. If the government wants us to respect José Martí, if they say we are all human, then first they have to respect us." The crowd burst into cheers and whistles.

"No war, no blood, peace now," Yosmel, aka Sekou, said as he took the microphone and led the crowd in the chant. The words resounded in the small space.

"Afghanistan has been the first casualty of the war on terror," Sekou told the crowd. "Who will be next? Iraq? Maybe Cuba? We, as hip hop, say 'no' to war and imperialism. Anónimo Consejo Revolución!" The crowd cheered. "Hip Hop Revolución. Put your fist in the air!" More cheers and whistles. The aging sound equipment came to life with a few static groans. As the beat kicked in, Sekou and Kokino, aka Adeyeme, began to rap, "No more war, no more blood, no more hunger!" "No more war! No more deaths!" continued Adeyeme. "Talkin' 'bout something real, this ain't a game / Prepare yourself for what's coming / I know what it is, stay calm, I take action." I recognized the phrases from Fidel's speech on the night of 9/11. As the world was yet again being subjected to arbitrary acts of American imperial power, Fidel's words resonated with Cuban rappers.

Here, in a mansion-turned-culture-house, technology courtesy of the Soviets, Cuban rappers were reworking the ideal of revolution to encompass the kind of changes they wanted to see as a local and global movement. The Hip Hop Revolución drew inspiration from the Cuban Revolution and from Fidel, but it was also connected to the motherland. And perhaps this imagined connection to Africa was what kept rappers somewhat outside the orbit of the state, even as they continued to collaborate with it. The ties of Cuban rappers with French record labels and African American rappers, even with fans in San Diego and Montreal, gave them a level of recognition. When black American celebrities such as Danny Glover and Harry Belafonte came to Cuba to meet with local rappers, it meant that they were somebody.

"Hip Hop Cuba with Africa!" the rapper Amehel of the group Profundo said to a serious and focused audience with its fists raised in the air. "Hip Hop Cuba with Vieques! The undergroun' protests Israeli repression of Palestinian children." There was a shout from someone in the audience: "Free Mumia Abu Jamal. *¡Libertad!*"

Note

1 Tricia Rose, *Black Noise: Rap Music and Black Culture in Contemporary America* (Hanover, NH: University Press of New England, 1994).

Cultural Cimarronaje

Afro-Cuban Visual Arts

> What many of us do via the arts is cultural *cimarronaje*. When Tosca sings, it is not a song, it is a cry; when Nancy Morejón recites with high lyricism, it is an arrow launched by the wind; when Mendive with his painting depicts a figure like Oggún, it is also a way of saying, "We are here"; when Chucho Valdés calls his disc Yemayá, it is a way of saying, "We are here." What I am doing is something similar to a painting or a rap song.
>
> ROBERTO DIAGO, MULTIMEDIA ARTIST

During the mid- to late 1990s, there was a renewed impetus for art dealing with themes of race and racism in Cuba. The exoticization of Afro-Cuban themes by the global market, combined with the development of a folklore tourism and the prioritization of the African presence in the Americas by international foundations such as UNESCO, gave a degree of legitimacy to representations of African identity, and Afro-Cuban artists took advantage of these openings to talk critically about race.

Afro-Cuban arts have been shaped by the history of the Cuban Revolution, Afro-Cuban struggles for equality, and an evolving and dynamic Afro-Cuban culture. Afro-Cuban cultures have transnational and diasporic roots, but artists are deeply local in their preoccupations. Afro-Cuban artistic production has emerged on the island both as a product of and in dialogue with historical processes of revolutionary transformation and cultural globalization.

Race Relations in Cuba

Racial inequalities in Cuba date back to the colonial era, when the Spanish colonizers wiped out the indigenous population and brought African slaves to the island to work on the plantations. Even after the abolition of slavery in 1886, black Cubans were denied equal access to education and faced segregation and barriers in employment, with greater concentrations of poverty. The Cuban Revolution of 1959 sought to remove barriers for Afro-Cubans in areas of education, housing, and health care, reducing poverty and creating social mobility for many Afro-Cubans.

During the early 1990s, the economic hardships of the special period led to a deepening racial divide and more overt racial discrimination in Cuba. In an era of increasing racial inequalities, the absence of independent organizations became apparent as Afro-Cubans found themselves without a political voice. Those activists who attempted to raise issues of racial discrimination were caught between a government that denied the existence of racism and Afro-Cubans who lacked a racial consciousness. But while Black Power groups had enjoyed less support among Afro-Cubans in the 1960s, black nationalism found more fertile ground in Cuba of the 1990s. The resurgence of Afro-Cuban struggles for equality in this later period was spearheaded through the arts, which is where dialogue about race was most strongly articulated.

Trajectories of Afro-Cuban Art

From the first few decades of the revolution, Afro-Cuban artists such as Wilfredo Lam and Roberto Diago sought to highlight black history and culture in Cuba. In the 1980s, a group of artists known as the Grupo Antillano (Antilles Group) challenged the modernist visions of Cuban art. The members of Grupo Antillano sought to build a cultural movement that could translate African culture into the Cuban revolutionary context. Their first exhibition was held in September 1978. By 1979, the group had seven core members, among them Rafael Queneditt Morales, Rogelio Rodríguez Cobas, Ramón Haití Eduardo, and Arnaldo Rodríguez Larrinaga.[1] The group participated in international tours and exhibitions.

Despite the early support of the Ministry of Culture, the Grupo Antillano gradually found its movement stifled. According to one of its members, Guillermina Ramos Cruz, ministry critics began to express some concerns. Art based on Spanish or peasant culture was considered legitimate, but art based on African history and identity was not.[2] A series of incidents, including interviews that were never published and television programs never aired, began to atomize the group. While the white artists associated with the Volumen Uno group started to receive international recognition with the support of the Ministry of Culture, the Grupo Antillano found itself excluded from national and international events and deprived of funding. The black members of Grupo Antillano found their culture appropriated by the white artists in Volumen Uno, such as José Bedia, who won prizes for works that incorporated indigenous and Afro-Cuban themes. Later, black cultural movements and collectives moved into the spaces opened by Grupo Antillano, and they confronted many of the same problems and exclusions faced by earlier Afro-Cuban artists.

In the mid-1990s, black artists once again began to take up themes of Afro-Cuban identity, race, and racism. These Afro-Cuban artists confronted a situation of silence about race issues. Since the gradual disappearance of Grupo Antillano in the 1980s, few artists had dealt with issues of race, with the exception of Manuel Mendive.

The exhibition Queloide I (Keloid I), organized by curator and artist Alexis Esquivel in 1997, brought together various artists who had been working on issues of race, including Manuel Arenas, Gertrudis Rivalta, Douglas Pérez, René Peña, Elio Rodríguez, Roberto Diago, and Esquivel himself. The word "queloide," meaning raised scar tissue, refers to the scars left on the skin of slaves from whippings by foremen. The artists involved in the exhibition had a fairly fluid understanding of race, as a psychological and cultural construct that can act as both a barrier and a symbol of cultural survival. Despite the lack of support from mainstream art institutions in Havana, Esquivel went on to organize another exhibition at the end of 1997 in collaboration with art critic Ariel Ribeaux. It was titled Ni músicos, ni deportistas (Not musicians, nor athletes), a reference to the social stereotypes that confine the cultural contributions of Afro-Cubans to music and sports.

The pieces in the exhibitions reflected various perspectives. Esquivel's work drew on the social and political significance of a rope known as the *soga*, which was used to separate whites and blacks at dances. The artist tied the rope in knots around his head, expressing the violence of racial discrimination and the restrictions it places on the individual. In the series *Queloides*, Peña presented close-up photographic images of scars on black skin, evoking the title of the show in a visceral manner. The marking of black bodies by powerful histories and social stereotypes is a theme in Peña's work. In another piece by Peña titled *Cuchillo* (Knife), the replacement of the penis of the black man with a knife was a comment on the fears and myths of black male sexuality. Manuel Arenas's pieces, *Carné de identidad* (ID card) and *Cuidado, hay negro* (Watch out for the black man), recalled songs by rap artists in protest of police harassment of black youth. In *Carné de identidad*, the image of a black man showing his identification card was at the center of the Cuban national emblem. One of the emblem's symbols was replaced with a penis, dramatically demonstrating the conflation of official documents with the physical body in the game of requesting an ID. In *Cuidado, hay negro*, which evoked the signs reading "Cuidado, hay perro" (Beware of the dog) commonly posted near houses, Arenas invited intruders to be cautious. He turned social stereotypes on their head, employing threatening imagery to reclaim the social existence of the black man.

The exhibitions offered a provocative critique of the notions of race and blackness being fetishized by global markets and the state-promoted tourism industry. Artists took a critical look at race relations in Cuba, but they faced suspicion and were advised to abandon the project because it was seen as professionally risky. At the same time, the exhibitions put the artists on the cultural map and created a certain space of legitimacy for their work. Ribeaux wrote an essay based on the project, which was awarded a prestigious prize from the First National Biennial of the Theory and Criticism of Contemporary Art and was later published in the art journal *Arte Cubano*. Through the exhibitions, a range of topics was debated, including the reemergence of racism in the tourist economy, the role and possible value of Afro-Cuban culture for generating foreign exchange through a more "dignified" tourism, and the entrustment of cultural promotion to white Cubans who are often ignorant of Afro-Cuban cultural traditions.[3] Queloide I both represented and gave rise to an emerging body of art by Afro-Cuban artists that sought to engage with sociopolitical themes of marginality, race, and power.

Another artist, Roberto Diago, presented painting in the form of graffiti. Like rap music, graffiti is an alternative way of writing the history of the city and telling the stories that have been relegated to the margins. For Diago, it is black history, culture, and voices that have been silenced. In contrast to official national histories which sought to subsume black identity, Diago's graffiti brought to the fore the notion of a black history. One graffiti painting produced by Diago in 2002 read, "Cuba Si! Fucked. Black 100%. My history." Another read, "My history is your history." Diago's graffiti demanded people's attention and raised the profile of black Cuba in a context where it was hidden and ignored. Like Esquivel, Rodríguez, and Arenas, Diago was concerned with the social conditions of race as lived reality.

Following the Queloide I exhibition, several of the artists involved began to create performances and interventions in public space. During the 2000 Biennial, Esquivel created a performance in the Plaza Vieja, the historic center of Havana, titled *Acción afirmativa* (Affirmative action). In the performance, Esquivel assumed the position of a street vendor, positioned next to a large sales rack containing only a black doll, which he had purchased moments earlier in a tourist market. Esquivel proceeded with a sales pitch, where he attempted to sell the doll to various passersby for more than fifteen times its value. One observer noted that Esquivel employed a pedantic discourse about the ideological value of the doll, saying that it represented black women who were most oppressed by slavery and was therefore more valuable than other items for sale in the tourist market.[4] Another critic noted the ways in which Esquivel sought to present his doll as "committed art," parodying the false aura of radicalism used to attract foreign buyers and dealers.[5] The artist related to me that there were a series of reactions to his sales pitch. Some people began to discuss with him the reality of racial problems in Cuba, and others bartered with him over the price of the doll. Esquivel's performance was both a part of the Biennial and a comment on the kinds of "radical" discourses used to attract foreign buyers in the international marketplace of the Biennial, as well as more locally in the tourist market.

The emergence of art dealing with questions of race from a sociopolitical perspective paralleled the rise of rap music as a voice for Afro-Cuban youth. However, visual artists were less optimistic about the possibilities for sustaining black voices within the arts, given resistance in the political establishment to their work. Religious cosmology and folklore had greater appeal in the global art market, but those who explored sociopolitical aspects of race were still excluded. The combination of an unresponsive institutional sector and the exclusions of the market limited the spaces within which black artists could express themselves. In the wake of the important Queloide I exhibition, there was an orchestrated silencing of the issues the artists had tried to raise.

Over time, a number of black artists migrated overseas or pursued international careers while retaining a base within Cuba. It became possible to speak more broadly of an Afro-Cuban diasporic artistic field, given the considerable amount of musical and visual arts production taking place outside the geographical boundaries of the island. This moment brought new challenges, as artists had to navigate the constraints of global art markets. But it also made available new possibilities for articulating Afro-Cuban visions in dialogue with antiracism struggles on the island as well as with artists and organizations in the diaspora.

Notes

1 Judith Bettelheim, *Afro-Cuba: Works on Paper, 1968–2003* (Seattle: University of Washington Press, 2005), 36.
2 Guillermina Ramos Cruz, "Grupo Antillano and the Marginalization of Black Artists," in *Afro-Cuban Voices: On Race and Identity in Contemporary Cuba*, eds. Pedro Pérez Sarduy and Jean Stubbs (Gainesville: University Press of Florida, 2000), 149–50.
3 Andres Petit, "*Queloides*: Eleven Artists Exhibit Works on Racism at the Centro de Desarrollo de las Artes Visuales in Havana," September 30, 2000, http://www.afrocubaweb.com/artevisuales.htm, accessed April 29, 2019.
4 Coco Fusco, *The Bodies That Were Not Ours and Other Writings* (London: Routledge, 2002), 139.
5 Cuauhtémoc Medina, "Una isla cada vez más isla," *Reforma*, January 3, 2001.

Elio Rodríguez

Of Joint Ventures and Sexual Adventures

Elio Rodríguez is one of the bold and satiric voices of a generation of artists who came of age in the crucible of the special period. Rodríguez graduated from Havana's Instituto Superior de Arte in 1989, the year that the Berlin Wall collapsed. His humorous and often profane artwork chronicles an era when Cubans struggled daily with multiple realities, dual economies, and conflicting ideologies. Rodríguez inhabits the proliferating clichés of Cuba as tropical revolutionary island to provide a searing commentary on race relations, desire, and power. His work has been showcased both inside and outside of Cuba. Over the course of his long career, he has exhibited at the Centro Wilfredo Lam, the Unión de Escritores y Artistas de Cuba (UNEAC), and the prestigious Fundación Ludwig de Cuba. He was an artist-in-residence at El Museo Francisco Oller y Diego Rivera in Buffalo and gave presentations at Tufts University and Harvard University, among others.

During the 1990s—the decade when Cuba began its foray into the global marketplace—Rodríguez was preoccupied with the encounter between Cuba and the West. This encounter is represented in racialized terms of the black/*mulata* Cuban and the white tourist, in sexualized frames of an alluring, feminized Cuba and the masculine, devouring West, and the ideological rendezvous of Cuban communism with Western capitalism. Rodríguez goes against conventional oppositions with humorous juxtapositions, such as the Tropicana-inspired halo of bananas and Che beret adorning the black man flirting with a white tourist in his 1996 piece *Tropical*. Lurking in the corners of his carnivalesque pastiches are images of vigilance, such as the menacing eyes peering over a neon Tropicana sign in *Tropical* or the Comités por la Defensa de la Revolución (CDR) insignia in *Con la guardia en alto*. State surveillance becomes fused with the voyeurism of the tourist as vernacular culture is prepared for consumption.

Racialized encounters are not a product of the special period, nor are they imposed from outside. Rather, Rodríguez sees the contemporary transactions of the present as situated within a long history of race relations. In a 1996 series, *Las perlas de tu boca*, Rodríguez draws on the iconography of North American cinema posters of the 1950s. One piece from the series, *The Temptation of the Joint Venture*, depicts a mulata woman locked in a tongue embrace with a black man. The trope of the "joint venture"—borrowed from the new capitalist lingo for "mixed enterprises"—is being used to comment on mixed marriages in Cuba. Cuban women have often been encouraged to marry men with lighter skin than themselves as a strategy for whitening. By contrast, the image, like Rodríguez's own marriage, shows the reverse racial pairing.

Along with the movie advertisements, Rodríguez created a fictitious company known as Macho Enterprise SA. The company is partly a commentary on the entry of joint ventures into all aspects of the Cuban economy, including the arts. But as an entity essentially "lucrative and for pleasure," it also alludes to the highly sexualized imagery that surrounds the global marketing of Cuba and the burgeoning tourist industry. The growth of the sex market has been one effect of this industry.

In the late 1990s, Rodríguez became one of the prominent figures in the exhibitions Queloide I and Ni músicos, ni deportistas. These two exhibitions helped give profile to the critical dimensions of his work. Rodríguez relocated to Spain in 2005 and like many other Cuban visual artists has moved back and forth between Spain and Cuba. Since moving to Spain, he has focused more explicitly on issues of race, which he now sees as a problematic present within all cultures and not just in Cuba. His exhibition Ceiba Negra, shown at L'Éscorxador in Alicante, Spain, in 2009, was an attempt to tackle and represent blackness as an identity historically subsumed within narratives of assimilation in Cuba. The Ceiba tree is sacred within Afro-Cuban religions. By presenting it in the form of a bulbous and protruding sculpture, sometimes even phallic, Rodríguez is reviving a sense of the bodily and physical presence of black Cuba. Given the trajectory of his Cuba-based body of work, ranging from commentary on racial stereotypes to mixed marriages and sex tourism, it

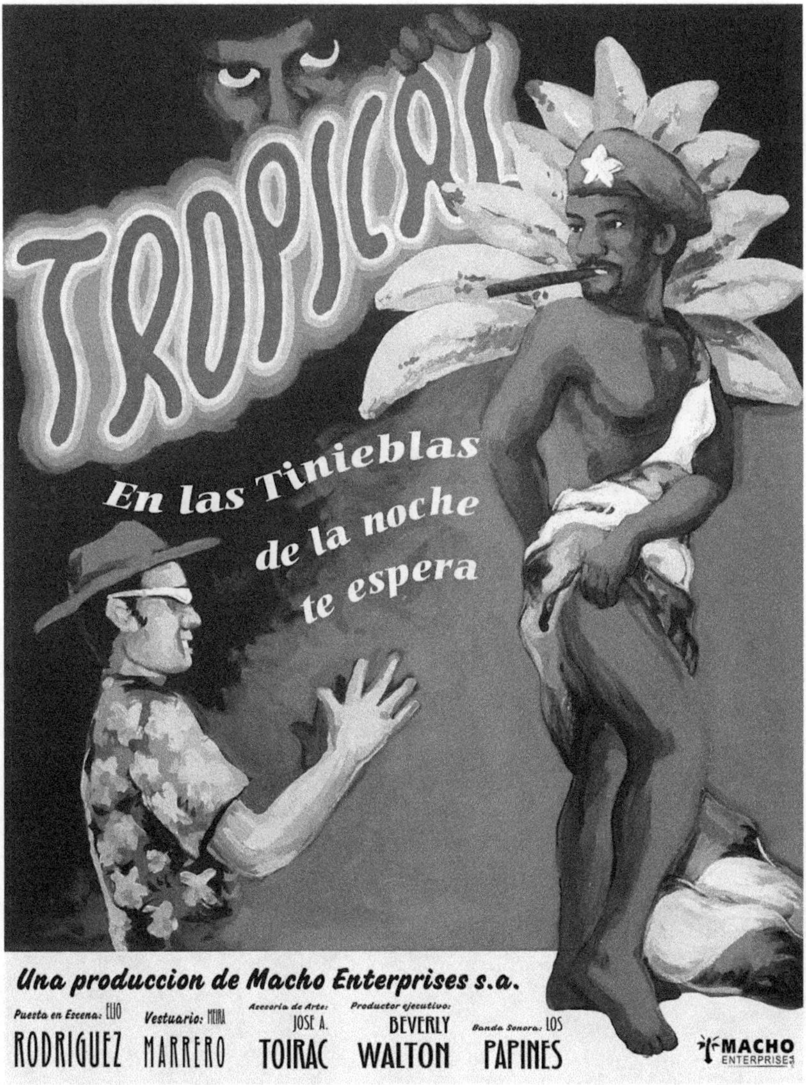

Figure 9.1 Elio Rodríguez, *Tropical*, 1996, in the series *Las perlas de tu boca*. René Portocarrero Silk Screen Workshop. Reproduced by permission of Elio Rodríguez.

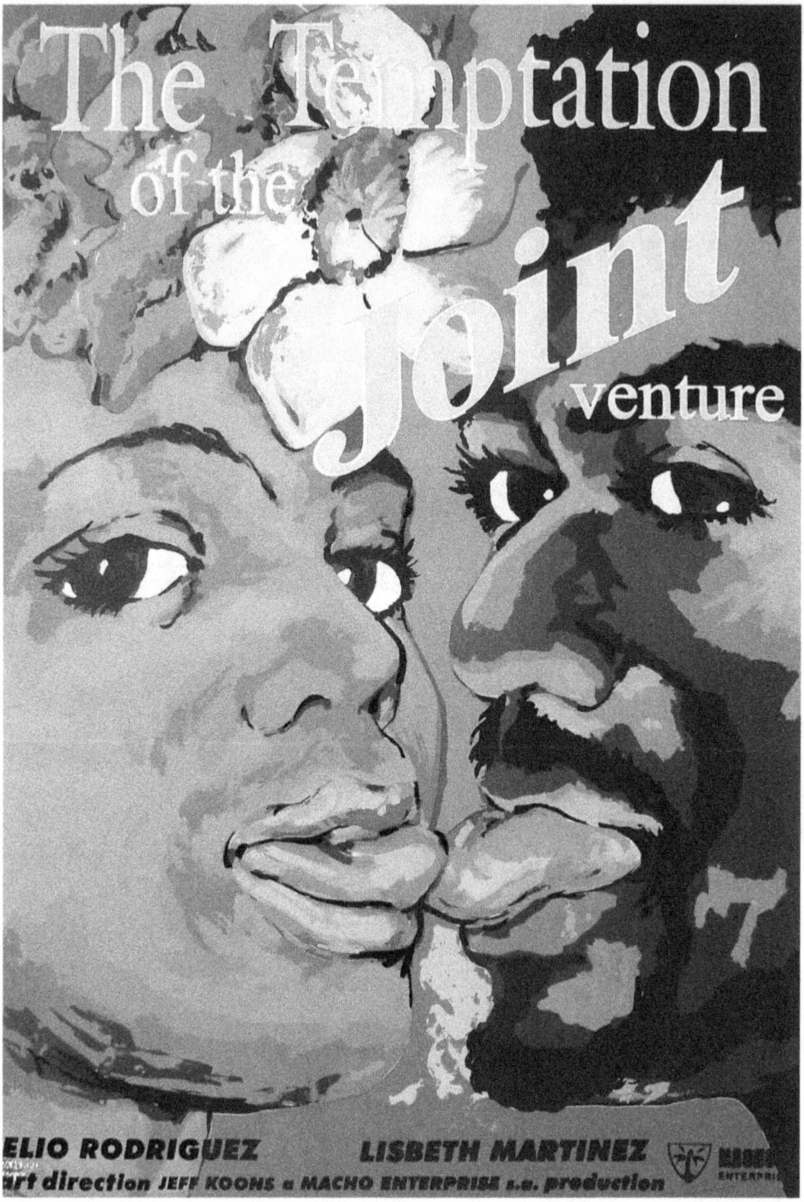

Figure 9.2 Elio Rodríguez, *The Temptation of the Joint Venture*, 1996, in the series *Las perlas de tu boca*. René Portocarrero Silk Screen Workshop. Reproduced by permission of Elio Rodríguez.

is not surprising that outside of Cuba he would have more space to ponder the nature of blackness as a submerged and often maligned category of subjectivity.

Note

This essay originally appeared in *Queloides: Diez años después*, art catalog, curated by Alejandro de la Fuente and Elio Rodríguez, January 2011. Reprinted with permission of the publisher.

PART II

NORMALIZATION

Netflix Meets the Weekly Packet

I go with you, beloved,
Although it costs me my life. . . .
A gardener of love plants a flower and leaves.
Another comes and cultivates it.
To which of the two does it belong?

MIGUEL MATAMOROS, "LÁGRIMAS NEGRAS"
(CUBAN BOLERO)

On December 17, 2014, President Barack Obama announced the reestablishment of diplomatic relations with Cuba. I was in the subway in New York City when a man starting yelling on his phone, "We're opening an embassy in Havana! We're opening an embassy in Havana!" The whole subway car was intrigued, and we all began discussing the surprise news, which was announced on television networks by that afternoon. Although the Obama administration had already been relaxing Bush-era restrictions on travel and trade with Cuba, the move toward normalization was a big step.

The era of normalization heralded a number of valuable openings and partnerships between Cuba and the United States. At the same time, democracy promotion efforts by the United States Agency for International Development (USAID) continued, with attempts to infiltrate the Cuban hip hop movement and the creation of a Cuban Twitter designed to provoke young Cubans to an uprising against the government. Unsurprisingly, both efforts failed and exposed the program for the farce that it was. Similar projects continued covertly even after normalization went ahead, showing this time to be one of both promise and ongoing peril, a point that was not lost on many Cubans who wondered whether they would be left behind as the winds of change blew through the island.

At the same time, Cuba was being buoyed by the emergence of left-wing governments across Latin America, starting in the new millennium. The island nation found itself with a net of supportive allies, including Bolivia and Ecuador, but there was an especially strong connection forged with the oil-rich nation of Venezuela under Hugo Chávez. Venezuela supplied Cuba with oil in exchange for doctors, built a fiber-optic cable to improve internet capacity on the island, and gave loans and grants to Cuba. Regional alliances also provided a symbolic boost to Cuba, which was now at the center of an anti-imperialist movement, after years of being ideologically unmoored.

During these years, the mighty figure of Fidel Castro receded into the background as he retired from the political scene due to ill health. Given his heavy presence in Cuban political life, there was much speculation as to how his withdrawal would affect Cuban politics. For those who saw the whole edifice of Cuban socialism as staked on the personality of its leader, it was a surprise to see that Fidel's passage from politics, and his eventual death, had little impact on the fabric of society. There were no massive prodemocracy protests in the streets, no long-awaited Cuban Spring. The transition in leadership presented a new scenario, as his brother Raúl had both less charisma and more market-friendly policies. But despite many decades of attempted assassinations and coups, the system proved itself resilient beyond the strict hand of its omnipresent leader.

This period saw many new and ongoing challenges, from difficult work conditions in rural areas and deteriorating housing in the capital, to the growth of shantytowns on the outskirts of the city to accommodate those escaping from rural and urban blight. But in an era of digital technology, even as internet access was limited and social media was heavily controlled, Cubans were inventing new forms of off-line internet, such as the Weekly Packet, to share information and create digital communities. Farmers used Twitter to publicize their plight. In the absence of a culture of critical investigative journalism, young people were turning to documentary making, using small digital cameras and cell phones to shine a light on topics such as the housing crisis. The antiracist movement also gathered steam in these years, with the growth of a number of small organizations in different spheres. Through the changing tides of political life, Cubans continued to find and invent new vehicles through which they could voice their concerns.

Cuban Rap

Where the Streets Meet Highbrow Art

Onstage is Instinto, a female trio extraordinaire. It's my first time seeing them perform in Havana. The divas are wearing shimmering, strapless dresses with high heels. As a salsa beat kicks in, they shake and turn, rapping lyrically, then singing in three-part harmony.

This is Cuban rap, where the streets meet highbrow art. It is an American-derived subculture that has flourished on the island despite—and, in some ways, because of—the United States' half-century-long embargo against Cuba.

In his first term in office, President Obama relaxed travel restrictions to Cuba and began granting visas for visiting Cuban artists. In August 2011, the Grammy-winning singer Pablo Milanés toured the United States for the first time since 1979. Many celebrated these changes as the beginning of the end of the embargo and an opening of Cuban society. But it's worth remembering that, despite the hardships, there can be benefits to living in a bubble. Islands are hot spots of biodiversity. And out of isolation, Cuban art forms such as rap developed a particular richness and vitality.

Rap was originally an import. In the early 1990s, young Cubans built antennas from wire coat hangers and dangled their radios out of their windows to catch 2 Live Crew and Naughty by Nature on Miami's 99JAMZ. Aspiring Cuban emcees rapping at house parties and in small local venues crassly mimicked their American counterparts.

"Just like you, just like you, nigger, we wanna be a nigger like you," Primera Base rapped offensively about their hero, Malcolm X. The group was known to sport thick imitation gold chains and fake diamonds—even though "bling" was a remote concept given Cuba's endemic scarcities.

But Cuban rap soon took on a life of its own. Unlike other hip hop fans around the world, young Cubans had little access to the latest trends in American rap, so they had to look inward for inspiration. With only two state-run TV channels, they couldn't tune in to the globally televised *Yo! MTV Raps* to see such pioneers as Public Enemy or NWA, and Havana wasn't on the touring circuit for De La Soul.

The embargo also kept out the key tools of background beats—samplers, mixers, and albums—so Cuban rappers instead drew on a rich heritage of traditional local music, re-creating the rhythmic pulse of hip hop with instruments such as the melodic Batá drums, typically used in ceremonies of the Afro-Cuban Santería religion. In the tradition of Cuban a cappella groups like Vocal Sampling, which conjured up full salsa orchestras solely through their voices, Cuban rappers made up for the lack of digital technology by developing the human beatbox, mimicking not just drum machines but congas, trumpets, and even song samples.

Cuban rap is also special for the caliber of its lyrics. Thanks to the country's excellent and free schools, rappers, although predominantly black and from poorer neighborhoods, received a high degree of education. Cuba's most prolific rap producer, Pablo Herrera, was a professor of English at the University of Havana. Rap lyrics mine Cuba's literature and history in their portrayals of the tribulations of street life. "I have a race that is dark and discriminated / I have a workday that demands and gives nothing," rapped Hermanos De Causa in their song "Tengo." The song reworked a 1964 poem that praised the achievements of the revolution for Afro-Cubans; a new generation was watching those gains erode.

The increasing innovativeness of Cuban rap stands in stark contrast to American rap, where the diversity of sounds and themes was eschewed in favor of a catchy pop formula with a focus on consumption. Hip hop originated in the outdoor jams and battles of the Bronx during the 1970s, and commercial distribution began in 1979, when the Sugarhill Gang's "Rapper's Delight" became a hit. Global entertainment networks promoted many influential rap artists, like Run-DMC and Salt-n-Pepa, but from the mid-1990s, there was less room for American rappers to experiment with unconventional subjects and styles.

Cuban rappers avoided this fate for a number of reasons. One was government support. Initially, the government criticized the "racially divisive" culture of rap, but after seeing how popular it was among the youth, the state soon came around. It began to support the annual rap festivals and then a yearly international hip hop symposium. In Cuba, many musicians were full-time employees of the state, paid a monthly salary for performing, composing, and rehearsing. Starting in the 2000s, prominent rappers also entered into this arrangement, freeing themselves to be creative rather than producing generic salsa-rap fusions to appeal to foreign record labels.

The government's interest in rap wasn't all positive, however. With state sponsorship came state censorship: rappers who criticized the government risked being censored on the radio or barred from performing in prominent venues. But censorship, like seclusion, can foster innovation. Cuban artists perfected techniques of metaphor, allusion, and ambiguity to trick the censors. For example, the rapper Magia López of Obsesión defended a song from her 2002 album that was about sex workers in barrios such as Central Havana by saying that it referred to capitalist countries. But when she wrote it, she had never been to a capitalist country. The song takes on a universal appeal because of the artist's need to dissemble.

This is, of course, not an argument in favor of state censorship or the embargo — which has deprived Cubans of basic necessities like food and medicine. The openings initiated by the Obama administration should be celebrated. But we can also recognize that some things, including the distinctiveness of Cuban rap, may be lost as the country opens up to a global market economy. It's worth remembering that imposed—even self-imposed—isolation can be a crucible for artistic creativity.

Note

This essay originally appeared in the *New York Times*, August 6, 2011.

Why USAID Could Never Spark a Hip Hop Revolution in Cuba

Between 2006 and 2007, I received numerous visits from two State Department officials at my home in Harlem, New York. I had just written a book on Cuban cultural production, with a large section on rap. I was never home when they came, so they left messages with my neighbors, telling them I should urgently contact them. When the officials finally found me at home one day, I agreed to meet with them at a nearby Starbucks. During the meeting, they wanted to know about my research on Cuban rap. One of the agents, a male, said that he enjoyed Cuban rap, listened to it frequently, and wanted to know what my favorite groups were. The other, a woman, pressed me for more details about my work in Cuba. I didn't give out any information. I told them that anything I could say on the topic was already written in my book. After this meeting, the harassment continued. I finally sought out a human rights lawyer, Michael Smith. He informed me that it is never advisable to meet with an agent of the government alone, and that if an agent should try to make contact, one should have a lawyer write to the agent on one's behalf. Smith then sent them a letter saying that I did not wish to speak to them anymore and that if they had any questions, they could contact him directly. We didn't hear from them again.

So in December 2014, when the Associated Press news story broke about the U.S. Agency for International Development (USAID) infiltrating Cuban rap groups between 2009 and 2010, I was not surprised. According to the AP, the US state agency paid millions of dollars to a Washington, DC–based contractor, Creative Associates International, to infiltrate the Cuban hip hop movement and promote rappers critical of the Cuban government. The Serbian contractor Rajko Bozic initiated the project. Bozic sought to provoke youth protest along the lines of the protest concerts that had challenged Serbian president Slobodan Milosevic. Bozic was focused on the Cuban rap group Los Aldeanos, part of a new generation of rappers who were much more outspoken against the Cuban government than earlier rappers, and spent thousands of dollars on a television program starring the group, *Viva Cuba Libre: Rap Is War.*

After a series of incidents, including an aborted concert and the detainment of Aldo Rodríguez from Los Aldeanos for illegal possession of a computer, the only Cuban informant with knowledge of the program tipped off Creative Associates that the authorities suspected Bozic of having links to the CIA. At least six times, people involved with the program were interrogated by the government. Los Aldeanos and other rap groups performed at the independent music festival Rotilla in August 2010. A few months later, the Cuban government took over control of the festival, citing USAID involvement. Los Aldeanos performed overseas for a while and eventually relocated to South Florida.

The covert operation included the creation of a Cuban Twitter known as ZunZuneo. In February 2010, a group of high-tech contractors, including the US government official Joe McSpedon, launched the platform that would be based on cell phone messaging to evade the authorities. The name ZunZuneo is slang for a hummingbird's tweet. The program, which was paid for and run by USAID, drew up to forty thousand unwitting Cubans through the distribution of innocuous-seeming news and music content, with the idea that political operatives would begin launching calls for political mobilization once it reached a critical mass. The hope was to trigger a Cuban Spring. But by mid-2012, ZunZuneo had vanished when USAID ran out of funds to finance the platform.

Infiltration is something that Cuban rappers have been wary of for some time. Navigating the legions of foreign journalists, producers, researchers, and artists has always been a challenge for Cuban rappers, especially during the heyday of the movement in the early 2000s, and there was sometimes a suspicion of people who didn't enter the scene through someone known to the community. But in the latter half of the 2000s, when many rappers were emigrating and foreign contacts and state support were drying up, Cuban rappers were more vulnerable to outside actors such as USAID, who sought to infiltrate the movement and manipulate it to its own ends.

The USAID mission to spark a prodemocracy movement of Cuban rappers was bound to fail for many reasons. To begin with, Cubans already had a movement—a multifaceted one that hip hoppers had built over several decades and that raised issues of racism within Cuban society, provided a channel of expression for Afro-Cuban youth, made connections with activists and artists around the globe, and had a long-lasting impact on Cuban cultural production. It was an organic movement built from the ground up, from the streets and the housing projects. Cuban rap is hope, and anger, and poetry, and no US agency could create that.

The Cuban hip hop movement was not trying to overthrow the Castro government. Artists found ways to work within the system, while making their criticisms in veiled ways, or even openly at times. The "Hip Hop Revolución" that they talked about was in dialogue with the historic Cuban Revolution, and youth put pressure on their leaders to live up to the promises of that revolution. Even the younger, more confrontational artists such as Los Aldeanos didn't see themselves as trying to topple the government. That was never part of their agenda.

"Prodemocracy" meant something completely different to Cuban rappers than it did to USAID. For Cuban rappers, democracy was about a fuller sense of participation and recognition within their society. It was about being able to express their ideas about racism, inequality, and the contradictions that free market policies have brought to an increasingly dysfunctional bureaucratic socialism. It was about trying to rethink what revolution might mean for the next generation and how they could see that in practice. For USAID, democracy promotion meant overthrowing the Cuban government and ushering in a free market regime friendly to the United States. Those two goals never have and never could be compatible.

The AP secured documents that revealed a frightening level of manipulation of Cuban rappers by USAID. As with ZunZuneo, the actions of the agency put Cubans at risk of state repression and threatened a closure of the critical spaces that rappers had already built and defended. The agency realized the power of culture to provide a powerful political voice for young people. What it didn't realize is that in a society shaped by successive generations of revolutionary projects, any attempt to engineer a US-affiliated movement from above was destined to be revealed for the farce that it is.

Note

An earlier version of this essay in a different form appeared in *NACLA Report on the Americas*, December 16, 2014.

Stories That Resonate

New Cultures of Documentary Filmmaking in Cuba

With Alexandra Halkin

Dissident Cuban blogger Yoani Sánchez completed a multicity tour of the United States in the spring of 2013, speaking at major universities and even visiting the White House. Sánchez became internationally celebrated through her Generación Y blog, which won her a place on the *Time* magazine list of one hundred most influential people in 2008. She was awarded the International Women of Courage Award by the US State Department in 2011.

Yet despite being hailed overseas for her dissident activities in the blogosphere, Sánchez has had less impact inside Cuba, probably because of the difficulties most Cubans still have in accessing the internet. Instead, the overzealous Western media attention to a few prominent dissidents such as Sánchez tends to obscure the highly critical culture that has developed within Cuba since the early 2000s.

Much of the media coverage of Sánchez presents her as a lone critical voice in a climate where the Cuban state does not tolerate dissent and where—as Cuban-American novelist Oscar Hijuelos claimed in his presentation of Sánchez in *Time* magazine—journalists and others cannot practice freedom of speech. While it is true that censorship exists in Cuba, there is also a culture of criticism and internal debate. But often, because many artists, journalists, and activists are not calling for the downfall of the government, they tend to go ignored or are sidelined within Western media coverage.

Digital filmmaking has been one way for young Cuban filmmakers to develop new skills in investigative journalism, often outside the structures of the state film industry and government-controlled media. They have used recording devices such as small digital video cameras and even cell phones to document their experiences. Some received professional training at the Arts Institute (ISA) or the International School of Cinema and Television (EICTV) in San Antonio de los Baños, but there were also a number of filmmakers who were self-trained. Many filmmakers sought to address the failures of Cuban National Television to cover the day-to-day realities of Cubans. These young filmmakers taught themselves how to tell stories that resonated with the Cuban public and to generate internal discussions that would improve conditions.

Historically, in the postrevolutionary period, journalism was under the supervision of the Communist Party–controlled Department of Revolutionary Orientation. But in the mid-2000s, young Cuban directors began working more independently via coproductions or raising funds on their own. Many of these independent productions were screened at the Muestra Joven (Young Directors' Film Festival) or the Havana Film Festival. Because of the lack of access to DVDs in Cuba, films were often copied onto flash drives and then passed hand to hand for people to watch on their personal computers. There is a saying in Cuba that there should be a "flash drive award," because that is the true indicator of the popularity of a film.

A few films made it onto national television, usually animations or films that did not present too great a challenge to the status quo. But there were cases where a film generated so much public attention that even though it had a strong critical edge, it was eventually broadcast. One example was Ariagna Fajardo's 2009 documentary, *¿A donde vamos?* (Where are we going?).

Produced by TV Serrana and financed by Cuban National Television, *¿A donde vamos?* was made in conjunction with a community video project that began in the early 1990s in the Sierra Maestra Mountains. The film opens with a series of scenic shots of the mountain ranges, dotted with palm trees and thatched huts. But amid the idyllic scenery, people are leaving in droves. They carry bundles, boxes, and mattresses on their backs; they pile their belongings onto horses and trucks. The film looks at the mass exodus of farmers from the Sierra Maestra Mountains due to an absence of opportunities for them to make a living.

In interviews with the farmers, coupled with footage of their difficult work conditions, the farmers relate the problems of lack of transport, the loss of animals and crops to theft, the devastation wreaked by hurricanes, the loss of money on coffee crops due to fixed prices, and the lack of help from the government. They are told that they need to produce, but they have no tools.

In one particularly devastating scene, a group of workers unloads bags of ripe mangoes to a site where they are supposed to be picked up by the government. The fruit sits, and no one comes to pick it up. Then the same workers are shown throwing out the fruit, after it has become black and rotting. Coffee also sits for days without being picked up, until it too goes bad and must be disposed of by the farmers who have worked so hard to grow it.

"People have lost their love for the land because they haven't received much support," says one farmer. Then he adds, cautiously, "I'm not sure if you'll be able to put that in the video. It might be difficult." While indeed such views may not have found space in official, promotional-type videos, in the new investigative journalism they are more common.

The camera pans across a series of empty and abandoned buildings with peeling paint; the name reads "The Politecnic Institute of Agronomy." A revolutionary slogan adorns the side of one of the buildings: "¡Venceremos!" (We Will Win!).

One of the farmers suggests that if the government were to plant cassava, corn, or other crops on the abandoned cooperative land and the land belonging to the Ministry of Agriculture, there would be enough food for people to eat. "Did the Americans say not to plant or grow things?" he asks pointedly. "No. So we can't blame the blockade."

At the end of the film, the farmers recall the historical debt that is owed to them by the revolution. "Farmers made sacrifices supporting the revolution, mainly when Fidel was fighting in the mountains," says one. He points to an older man gathering wood behind him. "Some are still here." It is ironic that the Sierra Maestra, a part of Cuban revolutionary folklore for the mythic role that it played in the guerrilla movement of the 1950s, is now the site of abandonment, where poor peasant farmers barely make a living.

This film was eventually shown on Cuban TV. After the broadcast, TV Serrana received a call from a high-ranking Communist Party official who said he was unaware of the problems that people were having in the Sierra and would see what he could do about it. The VI Communist Party Congress held in April 2011 declared agriculture and food production to be matters of national security, and farmers in the Sierra Maestra received assistance with their tools, were paid higher prices for their produce, and saw improved distribution.

At the Young Directors' Festival held in Havana in April 2013, Marcelo Martín premiered his new film, *Elena*, about the collapse of an old residential building in Central Havana where he grew up. Martín conducted interviews with workers and residents who showed him their deteriorated homes, which were plagued by leaks and contaminated with raw sewage from broken pipes. One older resident walked on blocks throughout his apartment to avoid stepping in sewage, and after undergoing major surgery he slept on a park bench while recuperating.

The brigades sent to repair the building did not finish their work and left the building in worse condition than before. The filmmaker calls the vice president of popular power to ask when the building will be fixed, and she lies and tells him the work will resume on Monday. He closes the film with a snapshot: nearly half of the housing stock in Central Havana is in bad shape, and 230 buildings in the neighborhood collapse every year.

This kind of investigative journalism—exposing official lies publicly and presenting the realities of people's lives—found fertile ground among young documentary filmmakers, but it often ran up against problems of financing and dissemination. Martín shot *Elena* over a period of three years on a mini DV camera using the built-in microphone. It was financed independently and received no funds from the Cuban Film Institute (ICAIC) or any other state agency. Interestingly, while shooting the film, Martín was working at the Film Institute in its publicity department, though he has since left to work freelance.

Young filmmakers pushed for the legalization of independent production companies and freelance producers. The issue was intensely debated. Under Cuban law, the activities of independent film production companies were considered illegal until 2019, so filmmakers were unable to register as a legal entity, open bank accounts, and so on. This made it almost impossible to apply for any outside production funds, independent of a Cuban state entity, unless you were able to secure a bank account in a third country.

Fundraising abroad was one solution. The US nonprofit organization Americas Media Initiative (AMI) provided crucial assistance by selling the films in the US and organizing university tours for the filmmakers. In 2013, AMI signed a distribution collaboration agreement with Icarus Films in New York. All of the Cuban filmmakers being distributed by AMI were given a Spanish version of the distribution contract. This was the first time any of these filmmakers ever had an international distributor and the first time they had ever seen a real distribution contract. Through sales of the films, AMI was able to purchase video cameras, laptop computers, and hard drives for many of the filmmakers who otherwise would have no real income from their films.

But there were also limitations to international funding, most notably because of the US embargo, which prevents US institutions or citizens from providing Cuban filmmakers with funds for their productions in Cuba. One example of this unfortunate regulation involved Cuban filmmaker Miguel Coyula. In the summer of 2013, Coyula tried to raise funds through the US crowdsourcing site Indiegogo for his new feature film, *Corazon azul* (Blue heart). Coyula successfully raised $5,288 but was informed by Indiegogo that, due to the embargo, not only was he forbidden to keep the money he raised, but all funds collected would be transferred to the US Treasury Department. Some of the donors received their money back after applying pressure, but many did not. The production of the film continued, but American citizens were denied the opportunity to offer their financial support.

The Americas Media Initiative sees people-to-people contact of the kind that expanded significantly under the Obama administration as crucial to bolstering the fledging work of investigative filmmaking in Cuba. Since 2012, AMI has organized the *Closing Distances/Cerrando Distancias* documentary film tours in Cuba, which requires applying to the US Treasury Department's Office of Foreign Asset Controls (OFAC) for special public performance licenses that can take months to be approved. Working with the Museum of Modern Art (MoMA) Film Department in 2012, AMI brought four US documentary shorts to four provinces in Cuba: Cienfuegos, Camaguey, Holguin, and Havana, where the films were screened at public cinemas, galleries, and art schools. Many audience members commented that they had never seen these types of documentaries or knew of these experiences in the United States.

In 2013, AMI brought US filmmaker Minda Martin on a tour to eastern Cuba. She screened two of her experimental documentary films that portrayed her experiences growing up in poverty in Arizona. At one screening in the small village of Victorino in the Sierra Maestra Mountains, over two hundred people showed up, including musicians and local performers. Not everyone could fit in the small video screening room, and the question-and-answer session had to be held outside. Afterward, Martin signed autographs and posed for photos. It marked the first time US citizens had ever visited Victorino. To this day, AMI still receives emails from audience members who were moved by Martin's work.

Given the stereotypes that exist outside the island of Cuba as a place where journalists and artists cannot practice freedom of speech, the growth of a culture of investigative journalism may seem either an anomaly or a temporary opening that will not last. In fact, it is neither; the island has long nurtured expressive cultures of filmmaking through its arts institutes and internationally regarded cinema school. The availability of new digital technologies has inspired young people to take those tools and approach their realities—which they don't see being represented elsewhere—with fresh eyes and perspectives.

Note

An earlier version of this essay appeared in *LASA Forum* 45, no. 2 (Spring 2014): 20–22.

What Do Cubans Think of Normalization with the United States?

In January 2016, the Obama administration announced that it would remove a number of impediments to trade with Cuba by lifting restrictions on the American financing of exports, relaxing limits on shipping goods, and loosening constraints on travel. These and other measures came in the wake of a major policy change announced by President Obama in late 2015. Normalization—the decision to restore diplomatic ties with Cuba—was welcomed enthusiastically by policy makers on both sides of the Florida Straits as the beginning of the end of an archaic isolation strategy with roots in a defunct Cold War. Although the US economic blockade of Cuba remained in place, it was hoped that these increased ties could provide the impetus for winning congressional support to end it.

When I spoke with ordinary Cubans at the time of Obama's initial announcement, they were much more ambivalent about the proposed changes. "We have to make sure that this is not another Pact of Zanjón," said an older Afro-Cuban woman, referring to the capitulation of the Cuban Liberation Army to the Spanish colonizers after the Ten Years' War for independence ended in 1878. Many Cubans were concerned about how the changes would affect their everyday lives, and they surmised that there would be drawbacks as well as benefits.

Several changes followed the restoration of diplomatic relations. During 2015, the number of American tourists visiting the island (excluding Cuban-Americans) rose by 77 percent. To accommodate this surge, the Cuban Tourism Ministry gave contracts to luxury developers and investors to build five-star hotels, resorts, and golf courses. The Cuban government received senior US officials, heads of industry, and executives from corporations such as Google to discuss possible trade deals and investment opportunities. These initiatives built on the reforms that had already been underway in Cuba for several years, including the legalization of small private enterprises, a new law allowing direct investment by foreigners, and a series of export-oriented projects.

Cubans were divided on whether they thought normalization was good for Cuba. A younger generation desiring greater economic opportunities, as well as entrepreneurs, small-business owners, artists, and others well placed to reap the benefits from visiting delegations, tourism, and foreign investment, welcomed the changes. But many of the older Cubans I spoke with—particularly those who worked in the state sector of the economy for fixed salaries, which averaged 640 pesos a month (about twenty-eight dollars), as well as others who had little access to remittances or tourist dollars—seemed to believe more firmly that normalization would have a negative impact on the country. Older Cubans specifically mentioned rising income inequality as a key concern.

When I first visited Cuba in 1998, the country was still reeling from the collapse of the Soviet Union, its main trading partner, which resulted in the loss of 73 percent of its international trade. The ration stores were empty, and there weren't many options for eating out other than a few state-run restaurants. In response to the transportation crisis, drivers were required to pick up hitchhikers at major intersections (a law that was enforced by the police), and Cubans crammed into bulky, pink steel vehicles constructed out of 18-wheeler semis, dubbed *camellos* (camels) because of the humps in back and in front. Local popular-music venues such as the jazz club La Zorra y el Cuervo and the Casa de la Música in Miramar were frequented almost entirely by foreign tourists.

By the mid-2010s, middle-class areas such as Vedado hosted a lively scene of Cuban-owned and Cuban-patronized restaurants known as *paladares*, and it was hard to get even a weeknight reservation at Starbien or one of the other upscale places. On a main thoroughfare called Reina in Central Havana, there were many small businesses, such as a bridal-photography store decked out with elaborately dressed mannequins in the windows, which was owned by a local woman who started it with her profits from sex work. Meanwhile, rural Cubans in search of economic opportunities migrated en masse to the urban areas, where they barely eked out an existence in the impoverished working-class barrios and crowded illegal settlements on the outskirts of the city. Whereas all Cubans, from janitors to brain surgeons, once earned similar salaries, in 2014 the government used the revenue from overseas medical missions to raise the salaries of some local medical professionals to as much as sixteen hundred pesos a month, while workers in some productive state companies and cooperatives could earn as much as two thousand pesos, depending on the company's earnings.

The divide between the haves and the have-nots preceded the opening with the United States, but some Cubans believed that the specter of what was to come—an onslaught of American tourists, trade deals with American corporations, free-trade zones, and foreign control of Cuban enterprises—would exacerbate inequality in a way that could become irreversible. This division was also racialized, with Afro-Cubans having less access to remittances and jobs in the tourist sector, poorer-quality housing that was harder to rent to tourists, and a lack of start-up capital for small businesses. As one Cuban antiracism activist put it, "Will Netflix and Coke negotiate business deals with people in the barrios?" One retired university professor told me that she saw normalization as leading to the demise of the socialist system. The state-controlled economy didn't work without Soviet subsidies, she acknowledged. But market reforms and trade deals with US corporations would threaten the system of socialized health care, education, and welfare that all Cubans, especially the poorest, depend on.

Others expressed concern that Cuba was trading its relative independence in the post-Soviet era for a neocolonial relationship with the United States. Cuban diplomat José Viera referred to a widely circulated nineteenth-century image of Cuba as a fruit hanging from the Spanish tree. At some point, it was predicted, this fruit would ripen and fall into the lap of the Americans. "For some Cubans," Viera added, "that moment is now."

One evening in late January, I stopped by La Zorra y el Cuervo to see Roberto Fonseca and his Latin jazz band. The small, intimate club on the downtown strip of La Rampa was packed, and bouncers had to turn away a long line of people waiting at the entrance. During the show, Fonseca addressed his audience in Spanish and invited them to tap out familiar rhythms and join in humming some well-known Cuban melodies. When a Cuban singer took the stage, she sang an old Cuban bolero, "Lágrimas negras" (Black tears), and soon had the audience—which included both Cubans and many returning migrants—singing along with her. There was a bittersweet quality to their words, which seemed to invoke Cuba's dilemma under normalization:

I go with you, beloved,
Although it costs me my life. . . .
A gardener of love plants a flower and leaves.
Another comes and cultivates it.
To which of the two does it belong?

Note

This essay originally appeared in *The Nation*, February 29, 2016.

The Repeating Barrio

The urban shantytowns have always been a source of vexation for the Cuban Revolution. During the 1970s, the revolutionary government attempted to do away with the shantytowns of the cities by providing housing, employment, and education to the poorest residents. The 1974 film *De cierta manera* (One way or another) by the Afro-Cuban director Sara Gómez shows a wrecking ball breaking up dilapidated shanty homes to make way for new, Soviet-designed housing projects built by microbrigades. But after the Soviet Union collapsed and Cuba was forced to turn to tourism and the global market, pockets of marginality began reappearing, populated by rural migrants to the city, the elderly, and others who could barely survive on depreciating fixed incomes. More than forty years later, the marginal barrios are once again present in the urban landscape.

Between 2010 and 2012, the legendary Cuban folk singer Silvio Rodríguez embarked on a tour of sixty of the poorest barrios, mainly in Havana. Silvio was one of the founders of the *nueva canción* movement of politically inspired folk music that spread across South America during the 1960s. Prior to the tour, artists of Silvio's stature had been spending more time playing concerts abroad, and Cubans complained that they hardly got to see local artists. Silvio coordinated the local tour, which included other renowned Cuban artists, including pianist Frank Fernández and singers Omara Portuondo and Santiago

Feliú. They attracted crowds of hundreds in the plazas and squares of neglected barrios such as Cocosolo, La Corea, Pogolotti, and Alamar.

The documentary filmmaker Alejandro Ramírez decided to follow Silvio on his tour, during which the filmmaker spoke at length with the residents of the barrios about their everyday lives. The result is the 2014 film *Canción de barrio* (Song of the street), one of the first documentaries to take on the troubling reemergence of spatialized poverty in the new Cuba. The film intersperses the lyrical songs of Silvio, accompanied by melodious flutes and his rhythmic guitar, with interviews of local residents. The mostly black and mestizo residents document in detail the accumulation of hardships that they face, such as the lack of proper sanitation, routine flooding, collapsing housing, and the unresponsiveness of local authorities. And yet, the characteristic humor of Cubans shines through. One woman points to the damage done to her home during the last hurricane. She shows where her kitchen collapsed and how her bathroom ceiling fell in. "There it is," she says, resigned. "I have to bathe under the stars."

In the process of touring and recording the tour, the artists and filmmakers had a close look at the struggles of daily life in the barrios. Water is a constant cause for concern. Some residents of El Fanguito live less than fifty meters from the river and are often affected by flooding. When there are heavy rains, the homes in Atarés, La Corea, Pogolotti, Loma Modelo, and Bello 26 suffer from leaks.[1] Conversely, in many cases there are no local water pipes or water tanks, so residents have to carry buckets of water for their daily household needs. When Silvio came to sing in Lugardita in May 2011, he discovered that the residents had been without water for many months. Seven months later, the barrio had no water yet, and Silvio wrote on his blog, "Why is there still no water in Lugardita?"

That these are not the favelas of Rio or the villas of Buenos Aires lends an added poignancy to the film: the residents are all too aware of the invisibility of their predicament in a country that has supposedly eliminated class distinctions. In popular parlance these areas are often spoken of as *zonas ilegales*, or illegal zones, for the lack of legal addresses, but in official rhetoric they are still referred to euphemistically as *barrios desfavorecidos*, or disadvantaged neighborhoods.

The government has always maintained that it is in a position to provide for the needs of those living in marginal barrios. But they have been reluctant to build basic infrastructure such as paved streets, sewage systems, and electricity. As one functionary told Mónica Rivero, a Cuban journalist who wrote a companion book to the film, "We are in a strong position to resolve the problems, but if we were to do any kind of construction there it would just encourage

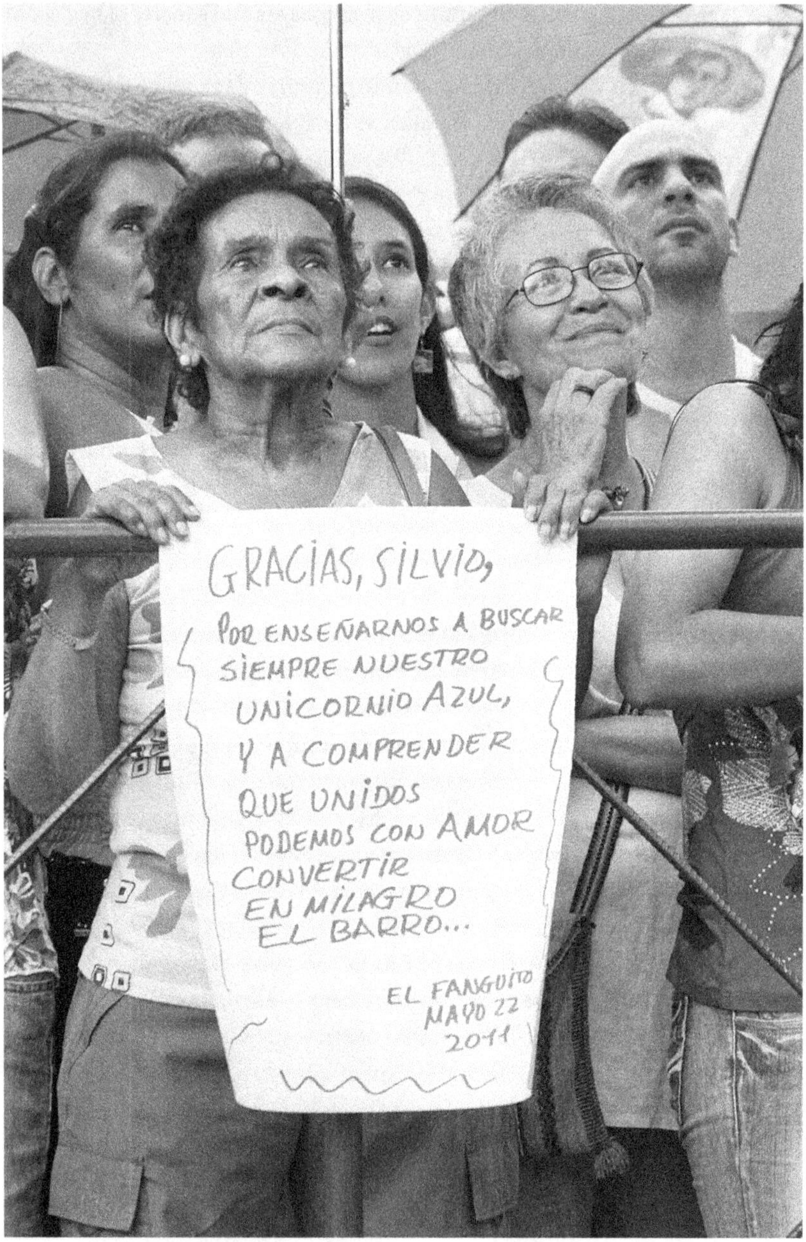

Figure 14.1 *Gratitude to Silvio.* Concert in El Fanguito. Photo by Alejandro Ramírez Anderson.

the phenomenon."[2] The official policy of the government and the Communist Party has been to limit the expansion of the barrios.

So the barrio residents, who keep growing in number, are forced to improvise in order to solve their problems themselves. In Romerillo, the roofs are a patchwork of wood planks, metal sheets, cardboard, and whatever other materials people come across.[3] An improvised bathtub in a garden is made from a large, oxidized piece of metal, framed by planks, cardboard, and nylon. Next to it is a house made out of wooden boxes, taken from the local cemetery.[4] There is a pragmatism to the work of scavengers. Surely the dead don't need their coffins; the living can make some use of them.

The film, however, shows an underlying paternalistic impulse of needing to bring "culture" to the barrios. Folk music and Western classical traditions are counterposed to Afro-Cuban religious-cultural practices such as Abakuá, which the film presents pejoratively as linked to violence and criminality. Culture is understood as Frank Fernández performing Beethoven's *Moonlight Sonata*. But the barrios have given birth to their own rich Afro-Cuban musical traditions, from the percussive genre of rumba to the more contemporary hip hop movement. Places on the tour's map, such as Parque Trillo, Regla, and Alamar, were key sites for the development of rumba and hip hop, a point that seems to be lost in the film.

Undoubtedly, local residents welcome having Cuban artists perform for them. But for some, lofty promises of cultural enrichment are overshadowed by more mundane concerns. "It's made a difference," says a young black man in tortoiseshell glasses. "The streets were paved because Silvio was coming."

The haunting beauty of Silvio's voice brings to mind all of the *nueva canción* artists across the hemisphere who were murdered or exiled by US-sponsored military regimes intent on stamping out their visions of socialism and sovereignty. Watching *Canción de barrio*, one wonders how different the continent would look today if the alternative social projects of Salvador Allende in Chile, the Sandinistas in Nicaragua, and the FMLN in El Salvador had been given the space to truly develop in alliance with socialist Cuba. And perhaps Cubans who fought for a revolution to bring them out of poverty would not be forced once again to live in poverty.

One elderly woman in *Canción* ponders why Cubans have to bulk up their coffee with *chicharos*, or split peas, when coffee is produced in Cuba. "And me?" she asks, poignantly. "Who am I? What is the point of being Cuban? Why did we fight for this revolution? For what?"

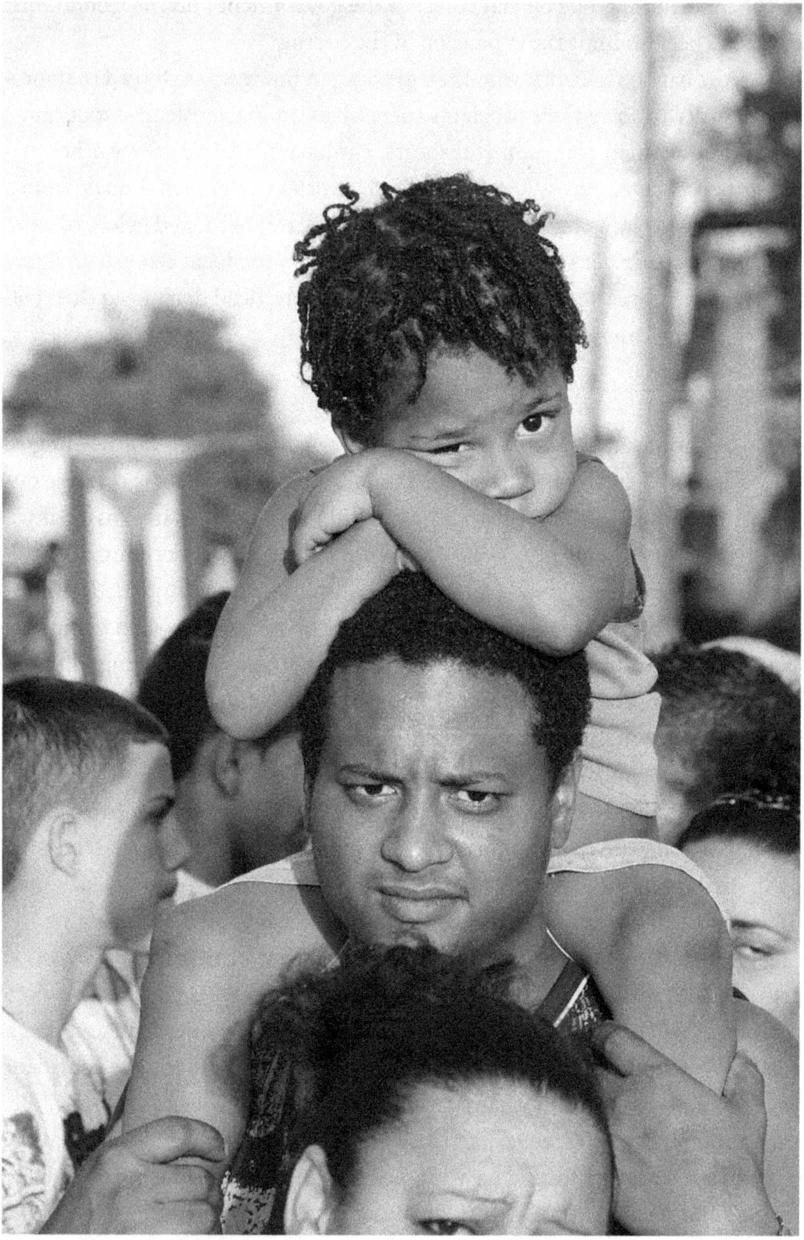

Figure 14.2 *Looks of the Concert*. Concert in La Corea. Photo by Alejandro Ramírez Anderson.

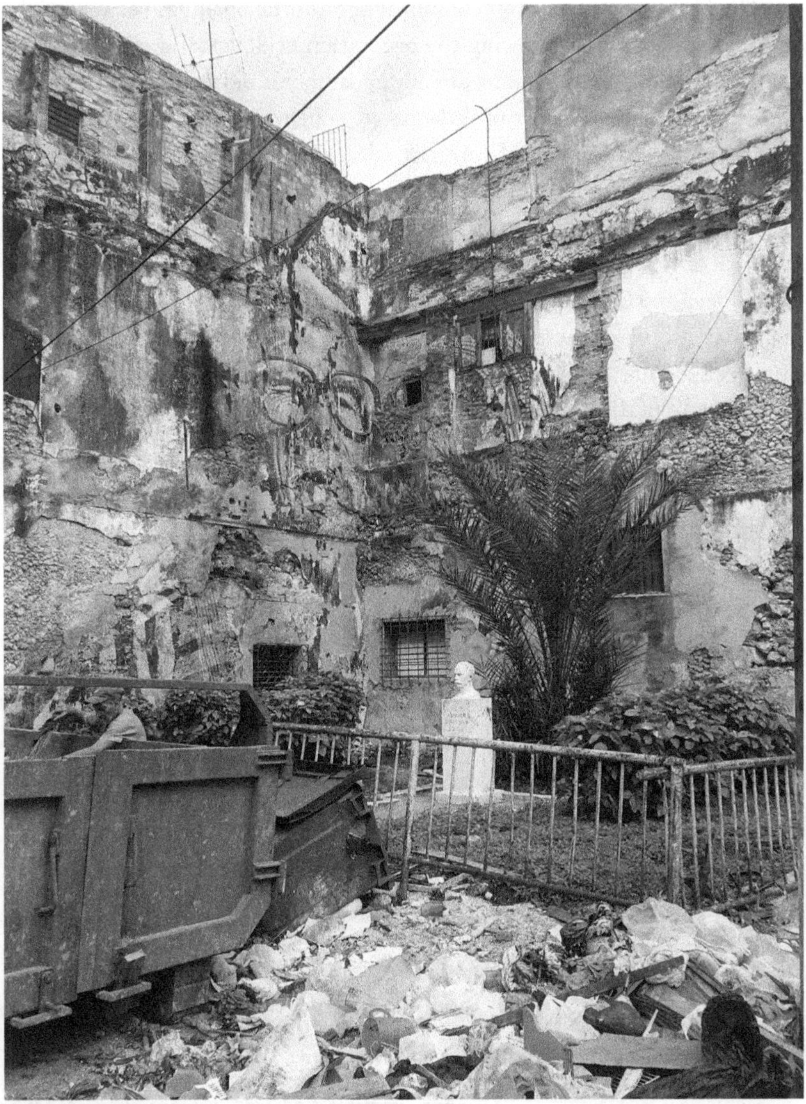

Figure 14.3 Garden in Los Sitios. Photo by the author.

The film was particularly relevant in light of the openings between Cuba and the United States following the restoration of diplomatic relations. Economic and social divisions were already apparent, as old colonial mansions in the leafy middle-class suburb of Vedado were bought up and restored by Cubans with access to a higher-valued currency, while the poorer neighborhoods experienced further decline. Likewise, as scores of American tourists donned head scarves and aviator sunglasses for rides through the center of town in a souped-up Buick or Chevy, Cubans who relied on these cars for transport to such barrios as Playa and Cojímar were forced to wait in lines to flag the few Cuban peso taxis that still made these runs. Amid the celebratory rhetoric that accompanied so-called normalization, *Canción de barrio* tells a darker story about those being left out of the promises of liberty and prosperity in a new Cuba.

Los Sitios was the site of one of the first concerts on the tour, and while visiting there I came across a lush garden fenced off by rusting yellow barricades. A mural of an unidentified older man in writerly black glasses, eaten away in large patches by the salty sea air, loomed over the oasis. Along the perimeter of the garden, a man scavenged through a brown dumpster, looking for recyclables. At its center, beneath a palm, sat a white bust of the Cuban independence leader José Martí, with an inscription, in Spanish: "The bad is accidental; only the good is eternal." Silvio's music has endured. Will the barrios?

Notes

An earlier version of this essay appeared at TheNation.com, February 1, 2016.

1 Mónica Rivero Cabrera and Alejandro Ramírez Anderson, *Por todo espacio, por este tiempo: con Silvio Rodríguez en barrios de la Habana* (Buenos Aires: Acercándonos Ediciones, 2015), 53.
2 Rivero Cabrera and Ramírez Anderson, *Por todo espacio, por este tiempo*, 110.
3 Rivero Cabrera and Ramírez Anderson, *Por todo espacio, por este tiempo*, 57.
4 Rivero Cabrera and Ramírez Anderson, *Por todo espacio, por este tiempo*, 6.

In Cuba, Will the Revolution Be Digitized?

Barack Obama announced his historic 2016 visit to Cuba—the first in almost ninety years by a US president—on Twitter, meaning that most Cubans would have to learn the news by some other means. At the time, only about 27 percent of Cubans had internet access, and not all of these users could access the full global internet. Many were limited to a government-controlled intranet through their workplaces. Key industries such as the banking system were only partly computerized, and simple tasks such as bank transfers were difficult.

It was generally agreed that Cuba would benefit from better telecommunications infrastructure, and during his visit, Obama suggested ways that the United States could help. In March 2016, his administration announced that it was lifting limits on the use of American dollars in transactions with the island, as well as permitting educational travel to Cuba for individuals, which would help with expanding digital access. Yet there was no consensus between the two nations over how the improvements to Cuba's infrastructure should happen.

In November 2015, the *New York Times* published an editorial calling on the Cuban government to partner with companies such as Google to update its telecommunications infrastructure and expand access to the internet. The editorial argued that the only thing standing in the way was the Cuban leadership's lack of political will. In January 2016, the US Federal Communications

Commission removed Cuba from its exclusion list, making it possible for companies to provide telecommunications services to Cuba without prior FCC approval. Shortly afterward, Daniel Sepulveda, the deputy assistant secretary of state and the US coordinator for international communications and information policy at the State Department, visited Cuba to discuss how US companies could help to connect Cuba to the internet. He reiterated that the main obstacle to improving Cuba's internet infrastructure was the unwillingness of the Cuban government to move ahead.

These perspectives downplay the role of the embargo in hampering Cuba's access to internet technologies. Presenting Cuba as a tabula rasa, stuck in the digital dark ages, fails to engage with the cultures of communication that actually exist on the island. These cultures could provide a strong base for constructing a self-sustaining, open, and accessible digital commons with robust privacy protections—an increasingly remote possibility in the United States, where ubiquitous surveillance is devaluing the internet as a public resource.

Milena Recio, a Cuban journalism professor and the Havana-based chief web editor for the American news website *OnCuba*, was a strong advocate for expanding telecommunications infrastructure on the island. But she cautioned that we need to talk not just about the internet but about "connectivity" more broadly. This includes the development of network-based services and intranets in administration, education, banking, and other sectors that would benefit from connected software applications. Rather than simply focusing on "going online," Recio draws our attention to the need for developing broader networks that could facilitate Cuba's transition into a digital era.

South America was connected to the global internet through submarine cables from the United States, but Cuba could not access these cables because the US embargo prohibited American telecommunications companies from providing services to the island. Under the 1992 Torricelli Act, which proposed US internet penetration as a means to undermine the Cuban Revolution, these restrictions were loosened, and in 1996 the embargo was amended to allow US companies to provide telecommunications services to Cuba. That same year, Sprint Corporation signed a contract with the Cuban telecom company Etecsa to provide a 64 kbps satellite at a cost of ten thousand dollars per month.

The costly satellite service made some digital access available for Cubans, but this was limited by various factors. Cuba was in the midst of a period of economic crisis following the collapse of its main trading partner, the Soviet Union, and there were no funds available to invest in internet infrastructure.

Further collaborations were hampered by the aggressive attitude of some in the United States, who periodically accused Cuba of cyberterrorism and digital espionage. In 1999, for example, Manuel Cereijo, an engineering professor at Florida International University, produced a paper in which he accused the Cuban government of plotting telecommunications espionage against the United States.

There were also embargo-related obstacles to expanding digital access. The embargo made it hard for Cubans to obtain basic equipment such as modems and routers. In April 2009, Obama authorized telecommunication companies to provide satellite and fiber-optic services to Cuba. Although the company TeleCuba Communications obtained a license from the US Treasury Department to provide a 100-mile fiber-optic cable between Key West and Havana the same year, the project was aborted because the company was not allowed to ship associated equipment necessary to extend the cable within Cuba.

Cuba's internet access has come from an undersea fiber-optic cable that was provided by Venezuela in 2011 as part of a program for regional integration and cooperation known as the Bolivarian Alliance for the Peoples of Our Americas (ALBA). Although limited in size, this cable made available high-speed connections for the first time on the island. In 2013, Etecsa offered a public internet service known as Nauta, available for 4.50 convertible Cuban pesos, or CUCs, per hour (the average monthly Cuban salary is 28 CUCs). In November 2004, the CUC replaced the US dollar, with the intention to unify it with the lower-value peso, although that has not happened.

In July 2015, the government opened thirty-five public Wi-Fi hot spots in parks and squares across the country, where Cubans could access the internet for 2 CUCs per hour. The popularity of these services reflected the strong desire for connectivity on the island. Despite the limited nature of the Venezuelan cable, which extended from La Guaira in Venezuela to the eastern coast of Santiago de Cuba, at least it made possible a higher level of connectivity for Cubans that was not dependent on the United States.

For many Cubans, the Wi-Fi hot spots provided their first access to the internet. A short documentary by Zoe García called *Conectifai* gives a glimpse into this public culture of hot spots. Families, lovers, children, and mothers cluster around the areas of connectivity with their tablets and smartphones. Their loved ones abroad show them snowy landscapes, supermarket shelves full of products, and roads without potholes. One woman sings to her lover, "Wherever you go, I'll always wait for you." Another girl shows off her curves to a man in Texas whom she has met on a dating website. A group of teenage boys text with some girls who are just two benches away. Even the older generation is involved. One woman reads out detailed instructions from her son in Barcelona who has sent her a phone and is explaining how to use it. Three older ladies keep trying to connect. They move around for better reception. The domain login cannot be verified. Finally, they cannot find the right card. But still, they all persist. As one man says, "In my opinion, the internet is a place where everything is. Where everyone is. If you're not there, it's because you don't exist."

It is often assumed that Cubans want access to the internet so they can log on to Facebook or other popular social media platforms. While Facebook is certainly integrated into the digital repertoire of internet-savvy Cubans, it only scratches the surface of the rich cultures of connectivity that have been gestating in the country. Cubans made use of the state-provided intranet as well as limited internet access to create their own networks for consuming and sharing information both on- and off-line. Those networks could provide an alternative to the corporate-driven World Wide Web, given the right level of support.

Although the nationally bound intranet was criticized by groups such as Freedom House for being a filter for the state to restrict what Cubans can and cannot see, it has actually been used by Cubans to develop local means of creating and sharing knowledge. One example of this is the Cuban version of the online encyclopedia Wikipedia, called EcuRed: Knowledge with All and for All (found at www.ecured.cu). EcuRed says its goal is to "create and disseminate knowledge from a decolonizing, objective, and truthful point of view." Rather than Cubans providing local content to Wikipedia, on EcuRed they create entries on both Cuban and non-Cuban themes for their own encyclopedia. EcuRed is run by the state and controlled by moderators who are government employees, but participation is open to all Cubans who are willing to abide by its rules of neutrality in reference to controversial political themes. The moderators enforce these rules and can delete or edit content and block registered users. Despite the obvious restrictions this places on content, it still offers Cubans relatively wide latitude to share information. As of March 2016, the site contained more than 155,000 articles, produced by tens of thousands of contributors.

Outside of the intranet, Cubans have created their own innovative grassroots networks. SNet, or StreetNet, is one of several informal networks of computers connected via makeshift Wi-Fi antennas and Ethernet cables. The collection of short documentaries *La hora de los desconectados* (The hour of the disconnected), coordinated by professor and web editor Recio, shows how Havana residents create communities of users on SNet such as Red Habana Este and Comunidad Sur Boyeros Cotorro, each with up to ten thousand members. Unlike the intranet, these networks operate horizontally, and moderators do not have the right to alter content. Although not legally approved by the state, these informal networks are tacitly permitted because of their clear prohibitions on pornography, sale of illegal drugs, and antigovernment material. Users access the networks to play online games, chat, and share television shows and movies. But as one user says in *La hora*, SNet is limited to those in better-resourced areas of the city like Vedado rather than poorer areas such as Regla or Guanabacoa.

One of the groups that accesses SNet is made up of mostly young men who play interactive video games. The gamer culture began among various young people in government-sponsored youth clubs. Video games were not allowed in the youth clubs because they were believed to encourage a culture of violence, so the young gamers began meeting outside the club. Through SNet and other electronic networks, they were able to link up their computers to play against one another in games such as *Star Craft* and *World of Warfare*. One young and earnest gamer in *La hora*, Ian Pedro Carbonell, founder of the Group of Electronic Sports in Cuba (ADEC), shares his vision of what he would like to see: "One of our main plans is to achieve a national festival of electronic games. Another is to have a national website, adec.cu. Also, we'd like to have exchanges between Cuban gamers and foreign gamers to raise the level. And, well, we'd like to reach a legal status."

Cubans also found ways to use social media platforms such as Facebook and Twitter, as well as foreign-hosted sites such as Revolico.com, an online classifieds site, like a Cuban Craigslist, that is hosted in Spain. Despite being blocked by the Cuban government, Revolico is accessed regularly by Cubans who use proxy servers to bypass the restrictions. Among the hundreds of thousands of items for sale are laptops, electric guitars, Samsung Galaxy smartphones, a bronze bust of Louis Pasteur, porcelain Chinese Buddhas, and the services of a clown called Payaso Refreskito.

Facebook users, known colloquially as *feisbukeros*, also find alternative means to access the site, although they can't share and download large files or use many other functions of the site. In one short, *La hora* draws on an actual story of a young woman who is on crutches after falling into a pothole. The film imagines what she could have done during her month of recovery if she had had access to the internet. In the fictional part of the short, the woman uses her time to develop a Facebook group called El Revolcón to share information about all of the potholes in the country. The filmmaker Rachel Rojas realized that the Facebook page could exist in reality, and she created "The Revolcón:

National Database of Potholes." Rojas recounted how the Facebook group led to more actual encounters with people in the neighborhoods: "We took photos, spoke with the neighbors of Central Havana and Vedado, and we gathered testimonial information that helped us to draw a map of the real necessities, many of which transcended the mere pothole in the street." Despite the difficulties for Cubans in accessing Facebook, the page had more than six hundred views in its first hours.

There is a Cuban farmer called Amador Sosa García who resides in the rural southern region of Cartagena, Cienfuegos, about 220 kilometers (137 miles) from Havana. Sosa, the subject of another short in *La hora*, is on Twitter, and in December 2015, I followed him on the popular social media platform. Within ten minutes, he followed me back and sent me a private message on Twitter thanking me for following him. Given the lack of connectivity in Cuba, especially in the rural areas, how did Sosa have the means to respond so quickly? How does he access Twitter in the isolated *campo*? Sosa was born in Cartagena in 1959, and after leaving to study computer engineering, he returned to the region in the 1990s to work on the land. He has a small LG phone that he uses to connect to the internet through Nauta. One of his son's friends helped him to set up a Gmail account, Twitter and Facebook accounts, and a blog. In one tweet, he says, "In Facebook, you can see images of some fruits of a large size and excellent quality, harvested in our small farm." In another, he says, "It's a difficult journey to access the internet. #Farmers need another way."

One cultural phenomenon that spans multiple forms of media and communications is the *Paquete Semanal*, or Weekly Packet. The Packet consists of one terabyte of data that is downloaded and distributed across the island via hard drives. The Packet began in 2007 as a clandestine medium with eight workers and expanded to an extensive business that employs about forty-five thousand Cubans and reaches half the population. It is a highly decentralized operation, with people in local barrios and provinces organizing their own packets. They sell parts of the Packet for as little as one CUC. Like many other kinds of subterranean digital culture in Cuba, the Packet mostly avoids controversial political themes and pornography and is therefore tacitly permitted by the state.

The Packet includes a range of materials. It has items downloaded from the internet, such as YouTube clips, Spanish-language news websites, games, music, computer-technology websites, and Katy Perry's Facebook profile. But it also contains pirated material such as Hollywood films, Japanese anime, exercise videos, e-books, and PDFs of *People* and other magazines. Cubans are able to watch the US television series *Breaking Bad* and *Game of Thrones*. Particularly popular are South Korean and Turkish soap operas and independent films from the remote Polynesian island of Niue. Another popular category is "Interesting Variety," which is a collection of all kinds of things from jokes to fashion tips to healthy recipes.

Because of the success of the Packet in reaching large audiences, many Cubans advertise in it, from small-business owners who want to promote their restaurants or English classes, to highbrow literary journals on the island. There is a high degree of customization of the contents of the Packet. For example, Cubans can ask their local distributor for a particular genre of film, such as French neorealism. The Packet also contains a great deal of Cuban content, including movies, magazines, and documentaries that might otherwise be difficult to obtain. Local habits of consumption are changing to fit the patterns of the Weekly Packet. Instead of tuning in regularly to one of the five local state television stations, many Cubans own DVD players with USB drives connected to their television sets, and they screen material directly received through the Packet.

Even if Cuba were to develop the infrastructure to make broadband internet easily available to its residents, Recio believes that the Weekly Packet would not go away. The Packet is more than the internet, and more than a video service like Netflix. Packet distributors are curators who provide Cubans with easy access to a personalized selection of audiovisual and print media from around the world. While Recio sees the Packet's reliance on pirated materials as a significant potential conflict, she hopes that it might transition into something more akin to Creative Commons, where freely available content not limited by copyright restrictions could be part of an open and plural public domain.

When we look at the grassroots cultures of connectivity that Cubans have built from the ground up—including horizontal and open-source methods of information sharing, using established platforms to promote social justice concerns—and the noncommercial nature of these networks, it does seem that these cultures could be the basis for alternative and innovative uses of digital technologies.

Most Western press coverage about the internet in Cuba presents the government as holding back its expansion for political reasons. It is said that the Cuban leadership fears that exposure to democratic ideas and the means of self-organization could be destabilizing for the revolution. Dissident groups and bloggers have argued that the Cuban government deliberately controls access to digital technologies as a means of social control. These blanket statements tend to conflate two different concerns: one is the fear of what the government calls "ideological risks," and the other involves security and privacy issues that have been endemic to the worldwide internet.

The Cuban government limited access to digital technology because of unfounded concerns about the internet as a tool of subversion. As social sectors within Cuba such as Afro-Cubans, women, LGBTQ groups, and others have become more organized over the past several decades, digital technology became an important tool in helping them to share ideas and reach an international audience. The highly controlled state media does not often create the space for these voices to be heard, and the flourishing alternative cultures of documentary filmmaking, rap music, and other genres that took on social issues had to create their own channels of distribution in order to find an audience. This included passing around copies of films on flash drives and uploading music to iTunes.

Many groups pressured the Cuban government to reduce unnecessary political restrictions. In February 2016, Reflejos, the platform of blogs managed by the government, shut down the blog of Proyecto Arcoíris, a self-described LGBTQ and anticapitalist collective. It was accused of "denigrating the revolution" by publishing a statement noting that the Cuban government had not apologized for the forced-labor camps for "antisocial elements," where gay men were sent during the 1960s. In a blog piece, the group stated, "The Revolution cannot move ahead while the right to free expression does not have sufficient tools that can defend it."

While the state censors and restricts internet usage in order to quell political opposition, the government's security concerns about handing over its telecommunications infrastructure to a company like Google are real. Particularly in light of the evidence revealed by Edward Snowden about how the US National Security Agency is using the internet for spying and to engage in surveillance of users, as well as paying telecom companies for access to their communication networks, ceding control over Cuba's digital sphere to private US companies could put Cuba at the same risk of insecurity that has occurred in other countries.

So what do Cuban advocates of connectivity see as the best solution for improving their telecommunications infrastructure? Recio suggested preserving the best aspects of the system, which keeps the infrastructure in Cuban hands, avoids the market as the principal distributor of connectivity, and has very little commercial advertising. As she explained, "I would like to see a state capable of being the guarantor, principal investor, and beneficiary of all of our infrastructure." In place of one company like Google supplying Cuba's infrastructure, she favored a plurality of companies, to multiply the zones of dependency. She would like to see the evolution of national networks that could promote development in a sustainable way. "We have to find a way to achieve the best degrees of connectivity possible," said Recio, "with as much protection as possible."

The way that digital technology and infrastructure evolve in Cuba could have vital lessons for the rest of the world. The global web is not the paradigm of democratic knowledge and freedom it is often made out to be but is itself a sphere riven by inequality, corporate control, surveillance, and privacy concerns. One hopes that Cuba will avoid the worst of these pitfalls and find a way to build a secure digital commons that taps into existing local and horizontal networks of sharing information. As Recio says, digital networks can provide a means to tell "the small stories of everyday people that you're not going to find on the front page of any official press in Havana, or in the polarized press of Miami."

Note

An earlier version of this essay appeared at TheNation.com, March 18, 2016.

Afro-Cuban Activists Fight Racism between Two Fires

On May 4, 2016, the Network of Afro-Descendant Women convened an urgent meeting of activists, academics, and members of organizations fighting against racial discrimination in Cuba. At the meeting, held at the Jurists' Union Center in Havana, the longtime antiracism activist Gisela Arandia presented a document calling for government action in response to a series of incidents on the island following Barack Obama's visit. These included several racist articles published in Cuban periodicals, an employment ad on Cuba's Craigslist site, Revolico.com, soliciting white applicants, and then a poster that appeared on a central street in the middle-class suburb of Vedado with a swastika and the note "Kill the black."

According to the Cuban novelist and activist Alberto Abreu Arcia, who was present at the meeting, there was much debate about the document, with some arguing that it was too conciliatory, that the events needed to be placed in the context of growing racialized poverty and renewed diplomatic relations with the United States, and that it should be accompanied by concrete proposals for change. Even so, many agreed that these events were not isolated incidents but rather made visible the racism that not only survived but had been strengthened due to an official policy of silence on issues that had supposedly been solved by the revolution.

During the period of normalization, Cuba found itself at a crossroads, with the specter of economic openings bringing the prospect of greater social inequalities, especially racial inequality. This moment had a parallel in the early 1990s, when the turn to tourism and global markets in the context of economic hardship following the collapse of the Soviet Union led to a deepening racial divide and more overt racial discrimination. At that time, black people in Cuba had no organizations through which to address racism. As the Cuban Revolution had desegregated whites-only spaces, launched an antidiscrimination campaign, and opened up avenues of social mobility through employment and education for Afro-Cubans in the 1960s, most of the race-based organizations that had represented them were simultaneously deemed unnecessary, and some closed of their own accord. The new millennium saw a reemergence of antiracism organizations across the island, with some fifteen groups forming in fields from legal rights to youth, culture, communications, and barrio-based community organizing. These organizations became vital during the period of openings with the United States, as Cuba was more exposed to a market economy and the potential inequalities it brought.

The fifty-one-year-old writer Roberto Zurbano has been one of the island's most vocal critics of racial inequality. In March 2013, when he was head of the publishing house of the venerated Casa de las Américas, Zurbano published an op-ed in the *New York Times* about how black people are being left behind in the new market-driven economy. His piece was titled in Spanish, "The Country to Come: And My Black Cuba?" After a series of edits, the *Times* published the final piece with its own heading, "For Blacks in Cuba the Revolution Hasn't Begun." As a result of this pejorative headline and the article itself—an affront to the leadership of Casa not so much because it was published in the *Times* but because Zurbano's byline included his position at the cultural institution—Zurbano was demoted from his position as head of publishing, although he still worked at Casa.

Zurbano's experience reflected the balancing act being performed by many antiracism activists in Cuba, who found themselves, as he said, caught between *dos fuegos*, or two fires: on the one hand a government that still denied the existence of racism and, on the other, black Cubans who lacked a racial consciousness. In many parts of Latin America, race has not been used as a primary marker of identity; this is even more the case in Cuba, where the postrevolutionary leadership declared that equality between blacks and whites had made racial identifications obsolete. That has made it harder to organize and mobilize Cubans along racial lines.

Yet in the face of these obstacles, antiracism organizations continued to grow. In 2012, Afro-Cuban leaders, along with antiracism activists across Latin America and the Caribbean, decided to create a transnational anti-racist organization with local chapters throughout the region. In September of that year, Latin American and Caribbean activists, with the support of the Cuban minister of culture, Abel Prieto, officially launched the Regional Afro-Descendant Articulation of Latin America (ARAAC) at the Ludwig Foundation in Havana. Leaders across the region believed that the Cuba chapter should be a point of coordination for regional work, given the profile and growing strength of antiracism work there. After the *New York Times* incident, ARAAC defended Zurbano's right to raise issues of racism in Cuba, affirming that the black population suffers disproportionately from poverty and lack of social mobility. Afro-Cuban activists navigate a tricky terrain within Cuba but are growing in profile and size.

Zurbano was born six years after the 1959 revolution. He came from a poor family of Jamaican descent, the youngest of five children. At the age of two, he was sent to live with his grandmother in the Nueva Paz town of rural Mayabeque Province, where she taught him to box and to read. Only one part of his family benefited from the revolution. The lack of education on his father's side meant that they were not able to take advantage of the possibilities opened up by the revolution for black people. His mother's side, though, was better prepared to benefit from opportunities for educational advancement, professional development, and access to material goods and services. Almost all of his relatives on his mother's side of the family became professionals in health care, education, engineering, and the military.

At the age of twenty-six, Zurbano became the vice president of Brothers Saiz Association (AHS), a group of young writers and artists in Havana Province. At that time, the association was considered irreverent and countercultural, and government leaders decided to remove him from the post. He was transferred to the military, where he served two years in the infantry. Zurbano defied the authorities and the regimentation of military life, spending much of his time in a cave used by runaway slaves in the hillocks of Managuaco. It was here that he developed his interest in Africa, reading novels and essays by African intellectuals. After leaving the military, Zurbano developed a friendship with an African diplomat and began to question why the strategic alliances of Cuba with Slavic socialism seemed to preclude a deeper engagement with Pan-Africanism and the Marxist writers of the Caribbean, such as C. L. R. James.

In the mid-1990s, Zurbano became vice president of the national AHS and discovered the nascent cultural movement of hip hop, where young black rappers from the poor and marginalized barrios of the cities were raising issues of racism in Cuban society. The Cuban hip hop movement emerged at a time when black youth were increasingly feeling the effects of racial discrimination in the post-Soviet era. While this generation had benefited from the extension of education, housing, and health care to black families, they came of age when the revolutionary years were giving way to times of austerity. Black Cubans were being excluded from employment in tourism, saw declines in their standard of living and housing, and were constantly harassed by police and asked for their IDs. Racism had become more visible. In this context, the militancy of American rap music appealed to Cuban youth. Afro-Cuban youth began to proudly refer to themselves as black.

Zurbano saw the rappers as the vanguard of the Cuban antiracist struggle. They were public and vocal about racism, and they opened up a space for debate and reflection about it in Cuban society. Cuban intellectuals such as the historian Tomás Fernández Robaina helped to develop the racial consciousness of the rappers by holding workshops on black thought. At this time, during the 1990s, Afro-Cuban visual artists such as Alexis Esquivel, Manuel Arenas, Elio Rodríguez, and Roberto Diago were also raising issues such as the manifestations of racism in the tourist economy. The establishment accused these rappers and artists of being "radical blacks," even as their work resonated both locally and globally. Over time, though, the rap movement won an important space, one that was helped along by prominent allies such as the American actor Harry Belafonte, who spoke personally with Fidel Castro about the importance of the movement.

While the antiracism struggle in Cuba was spurred by the efforts of the younger generation, its leadership also includes an older generation of black Cubans who remember the prerevolutionary years and view the current manifestation of racism with a different lens. These Cubans, mostly older professionals, recall the hardships of the pre-Castro era and take pride in their advances under the revolution, even as they seek to educate others about the need for a racial consciousness in the ongoing fight against racism.

Norma Guillard, in her seventies, came from a poor family in the eastern province of Santiago de Cuba. Her parents, a dressmaker and a tailor, had only an elementary education. The oldest of five children, Guillard was put in charge of her siblings when her mother left the house early in the morning to go to her factory. Guillard was thirteen at the time of the revolution, and at the age of fifteen, she joined the Conrado Benítez Brigade and became a literacy teacher. She was one of 105,000 youth who left their homes and went into the countryside, where 76 percent of the population was illiterate. Guillard recalls that it was a difficult moment; the US government was launching repeated of-

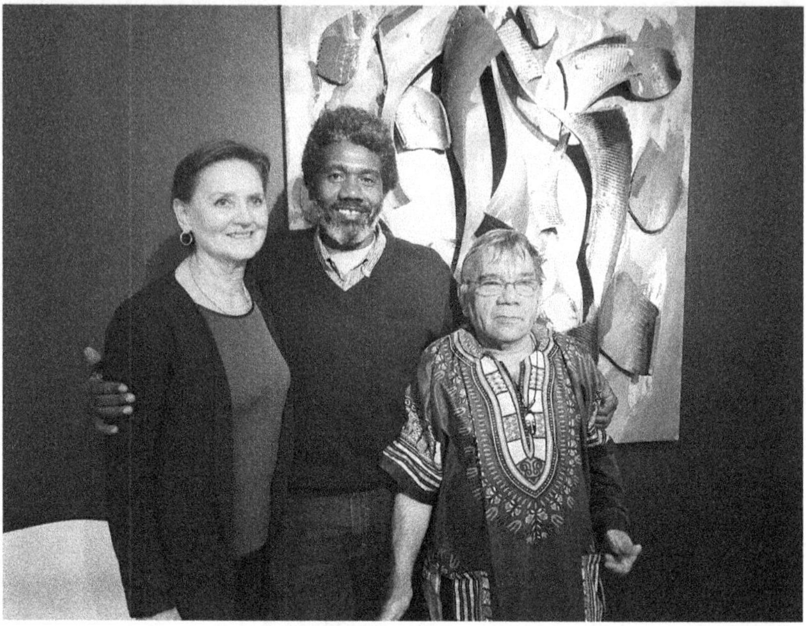

Figure 16.1 Julie Skurski, Roberto Zurbano, and Tomás Fernández Robaina. Photo by the author.

fensives to try to overthrow the newly installed Cuban government. Guillard was placed in the zone of Aguacate in Guantánamo, very far from her home. A counterrevolutionary insurgency occurred in the zone that killed a member of her brigade.

Guillard was rejected in her first home placement because of the color of her skin and was then placed with a mixed-race family. Despite the racism and hardships of rural life, the literacy campaign provided her with a kind of liberation from the constraints of social norms and gender expectations. After her placement ended, she went to Havana on a scholarship to study Russian. Housed with other students in the homes of wealthy exiles who had left the country after the revolution, she encountered the machismo of male students who wanted their female counterparts to wash and iron their clothes, which Guillard refused to do.

Guillard went on to become a social psychologist, with a focus on women's empowerment, antiracism, and LGBTQ activism. In the mid-1990s, she was one of the pioneers of a small network of women known as Magín (Image), which sought to engage in feminist activism and advocacy outside the direct control of the state-sanctioned women's federation. In the midst of the post-Soviet eco-

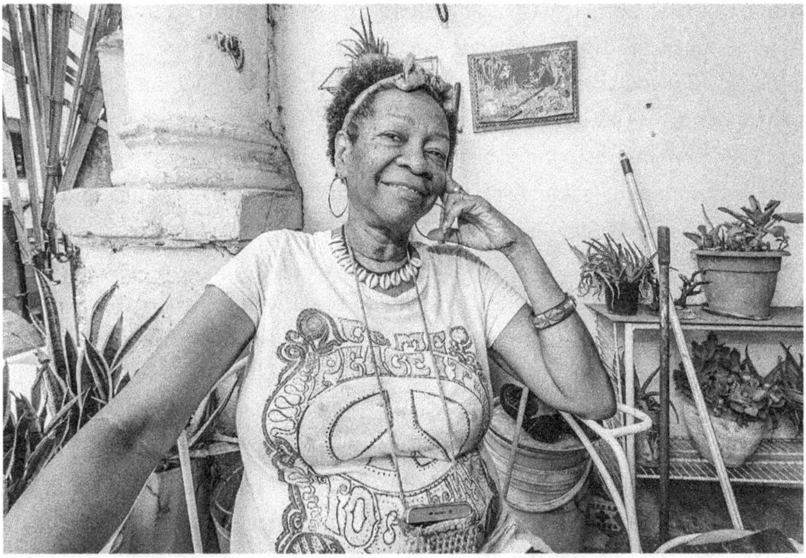

Figure 16.2 Norma Guillard. Photo by Matt Rogers.

nomic crisis, these activists found the federation—and its lack of a feminist perspective—unequipped to deal with issues such as the revival of sex tourism, the growing gender gap, and the negative portrayals of women in the media. The women activists promoted certain radical perspectives on gender and sexuality in Cuban society, such as the rights of women to engage in sex work as long as they retained their dignity and self-respect. After operating for a few years, Magín was dissolved by the Communist Party in 1996; this was part of a broader crackdown on independent groups that year but was also due to the government's fear that women organizing independently presented a risk of division in Cuban society.

In the new millennium, this experience was to be repeated with the antiracist organization Color Cubano (Cuban Color), which was started by the National Union of Writers and Artists of Cuba (UNEAC). Guillard participated in activities of the organization, although she was not part of the leadership. Zurbano joined it in 2002. As the organization reached a moment of intense activism in the mid-2000s, the Communist Party put pressure on UNEAC, which eventually dissolved Color Cubano and created a new organization, Comisión Aponte, from which several of the original antiracism leaders were excluded.

In spite of these setbacks, antiracism activists continued to find spaces to work. Guillard directed the Section of Identities and Diversity in Communication of the Cuban Society of Psychology, which provided a venue for discussions about racial discrimination. And it was around this time that Zurbano joined the Casa de las Américas as director of the publishing house, where he edited dozens of titles by black authors from Cuba and around the region.

The contemporary antiracism struggle in Cuba is a product of this history. It is multigenerational and transnational. The groups that have emerged in the period of the new millennium span from the urban centers of Havana to the eastern region of Santiago de Cuba. The spaces for their social activism are still limited, but leaders, many of them black women, are making efforts to engage Cubans from a range of social backgrounds and in multiple settings, from policy to activism.

In November 2012, the Red Barrial Afrodescendiente (Barrio Network of Afro-Descendants) was started in the Havana barrio Balcón Arimao. The organization was founded by three women, Maritza López, Hildelisa Leal, and Damayanti Matos, with the aim of supporting antiracist activism in the marginalized barrios of Havana and creating projects to promote the economic vitality and solidarity of the majority-black residents. The Red Barrial is based on a horizontal style of organizing, local leadership development, and collective decision making, drawing on ideas of popular education and taking inspiration from radical Brazilian educator Paulo Freire and Martin Luther King Jr. Working closely with the female-led organization Grupo Afrocubanas, the Red Barrial seeks to bring together local barrio residents—mechanics, religious leaders, architects, and doctors—to discuss old and new forms of racial discrimination and ways to fight them.

Another project that began in 2012 is the legal-cultural organization Alianza Unidad Racial (Racial Unity Alliance). Started by the lawyer Deyni Terri Abreu, it focuses on civil rights, citizen education, and penal rights. The Alianza offers free legal workshops and has won several antidiscrimination cases, including one of a black man who had suffered employment discrimination. It has also defended black Cubans in cases of excessive police harassment. While about 10 percent of Cubans self-identify as black in the country's census, the Cuban social scientist Rosa Campoalegre argues that they are greatly overrepresented in the criminal justice and penal systems. Black youth are frequently stopped by police on the streets and arrested without cause. As a legal organization, the Alianza has faced some challenges, given that the state-approved national organization of lawyers is the body usually required to provide legal representation in court cases. As a result, the Alianza has generally been limited to court accompaniment, legal advice, and cultural work, such as training people in how to dress and present themselves in court.

These various organizations come together under the umbrella group ARAAC, which counts on the participation of many longtime antiracism activists in Cuba, including Zurbano, Guillard, Arandia, and Abreu, as well as the historian Robaina. Arandia saw the formation of the Cuban chapter of ARAAC in 2012 as a major advance in the struggle for racial equality in Cuba. While ARAAC evolved out of the earlier struggles on the island, Arandia also saw it as marking a different moment, when various groups could come together in a new structure to change public policy, reach out to broader social sectors, and build alliances with Afro-descendant groups across Latin America and the Caribbean.

In response to official rhetoric, which holds that talking about race divides the nation, the activists of ARAAC argue instead that it is silence about race that creates division. Activists have been bolder in staking out their autonomy from the state. Gisela Morales (Giselita), who stepped down from a paid position in ARAAC, argued at the May 4 meeting that she did not want to take money from the state and that ARAAC should be independent: "If the citizens decide to meet, they don't have to ask permission from the state, and no one can dissolve a process that the citizens decide to take forward."

Spurred by the Black Lives Matter movement in the United States, we are witnessing a moment of heightened antiracist struggle globally. Groups such as Warriors of the Aboriginal Resistance (WAR) in Australia and the New Urban Collective in Amsterdam have taken inspiration from Black Lives Matter while highlighting their own unique struggles. This moment presents new opportunities for the antiracist movement in Cuba. Cuban activists recognize the differences, of course: that while police brutality and murder of black youth are all too common in the United States, in Cuba police rarely use weapons or kill unarmed black people. But the disproportionate surveillance and harassment of black youth on the island does provide grounds for transnational solidarity. The other opening came from the United Nations–sponsored International Decade for People of African Descent, which began in January 2015 under the themes of recognition, justice, and development. The resulting conversations, gatherings, and networks have given momentum to antiracism organizations and their demands in Cuba.

Antiracism organizations in Cuba may fall outside the radar of the international news media because they don't fit the profile of the typical dissident groups, such as those calling for freedom of speech and denouncing the government. Rather, groups such as ARAAC are part of a lineage of activism that exists within the parameters of the Cuban Revolution, recognizing its progress in fighting structural discrimination and seeking to preserve the social and economic benefits that Afro-Cubans have won. Their allegiance to the ideals of the revolution has helped Afro-Cuban activists to navigate a path for independent dialogue within the constraints of the political system. But the threat of closure or sanction is always a possibility, as is the reality of racist backlash. One article published on the Cuban website El Heraldo Cubano denied the existence of racism in Cuba and attacked the Alianza Unidad Racial and another organization, Cofradía de la Negritud (Brotherhood of Blackness), as counterrevolutionaries funded by the US government. But these organizations and activists openly define themselves as anticapitalist, anti-imperialist, and decolonizing. That does not endear them to the kinds of US democracy-promotion programs sponsored by USAID and the Obama administration.

The openings between Cuba and the United States created a greater need for these antiracism organizations on the island, as an expanding market economy generated increased racial and economic inequalities. Given the concentration of black Cubans in substandard housing, their lack of access to capital, including remittances from abroad, and the prevalence of racist norms in hiring for the tourism industry, Afro-Cubans are much more poorly placed to take advantage of openings for social mobility and economic improvement. Black-led antiracism organizations provide the best chance for ensuring that Afro-Cubans are not left behind.

Note

This essay originally appeared at TheNation.com, May 24, 2016.

Black Diasporic Dialogues in Post-Soviet Cuba

Solidarity between Cuba and African Americans has a fairly long history. In the postrevolutionary period, Cuban leaders sought to reach out directly to Black Power movements, and Cuba served as a haven for black militants fleeing political persecution from the United States government. Black Americans looked to Cuba as a country that was empowering its black population through a revolution. And Cuba was hailed for its progress on issues of racial inequality by certain sectors of African Americans. In the new millennium, particularly given the growth of Afro-Cuban organizations on the island, there have been more initiatives to establish direct linkages between Afro-Cubans and African Americans—beyond the diplomatic efforts of states and the political priorities of the revolution.

Soon after the triumph of the revolution, the Cuban revolutionary leadership began to reach out to African American intellectuals and leaders as allies to combat the propaganda of the US government and create a counterpoint to the predominantly white and upper-class Cuban exile community.[1] Through government-sponsored tours, black American leaders were able to see firsthand the struggle that was being waged against racism through state-led efforts at desegregation, income redistribution, and antidiscrimination policies. During the 1960s, the Castro government deepened ties with Black Power groups such as the Black Panther Party. Militants including Robert F. Williams, Eldridge

Cleaver, and Huey Newton visited the island, and others, such as Assata Shakur, were given political asylum in Cuba.

The Cuban government's internationalist focus and its critique of imperialism fit well with the political program of Black Power movements. Both believed that the dismantling of capitalism was key to the liberation of all peoples, and the Cuban Revolution gave the Black Panthers a chance to see their theoretical ideas in practice. However, many of these militants became frustrated with the integrationist agenda of the Cuban government. Black Power advocates such as Williams and Cleaver believed that black people needed to organize independently, at a time when the black press and Afro-Cuban clubs within Cuba were being dissolved or closed themselves down because of widely held beliefs promoted by the revolutionary leadership that racial equality depended on integrating Afro-Cubans into Cuban society and even eradicating the very construct of race. In general, the alliance between Cuba and African Americans during the first three decades of the revolution was a tenuous one, and it was largely conducted through diplomatic channels in the service of Cuba's foreign policy.

Since the collapse of the Soviet Union, Afro-Cuban organizations on the island have reemerged, particularly given the differentiated effects that tourism and market reforms have had in deepening Cuba's growing racial divide. In the second decade of the new millennium there were some twenty Afro-Cuban organizations in existence, which formed part of an increasingly vibrant and pluralist antiracist movement that also included the hip hop movement and Afro-Cuban religious organizations. Through digital technology, these movements were reaching broader regional and international publics and increasing the possibilities for "person-to-person" contact. Additionally, there were greater moves from both African American and Afro-Cuban leaders to establish direct connections between grassroots groups, and these initiatives have been especially prominent in areas of culture and music, with hopes of also establishing economic ties, such as links between black businesses in both countries.

The African American organization TransAfrica was at center of these efforts in the early post-Soviet era. Starting in the mid-1990s, TransAfrica began to initiate a dialogue with Cuban institutions. Prominent black actors Harry Belafonte and Danny Glover, writer Alice Walker, and others began to visit the island; shortly thereafter, they initiated contact with Cuban activists involved in the island's antiracist movement.[2] These black American artists and intellectuals helped to open an important space for antiracist movements within Cuba. For instance, Belafonte addressed the importance of the Cuban hip hop movement with Fidel Castro, heralding an era of greater openness toward rap artists.

Another important source of contemporary diasporic dialogue was the Black August Hip Hop Project, which contributed to the development of global hip hop culture by promoting contact between international communities and awareness of the social and political issues faced by those communities. The collective arranged for black American emcees Paris, Common, dead prez, Mos Def, and Talib Kweli to perform at the annual Cuban hip hop festivals in Alamar during the late 1990s. Black August concerts held in New York, meanwhile, raised money for the Cuban hip hop movement, including funding for the Cuban festivals.

American rappers spoke a language of black militancy that was appealing to young Cubans. The rapper Sekuo Umoja of the group Anónimo Consejo said to me, "We had the same vision as rappers such as Paris, who was one of the first to come to Cuba. His music drew my attention, because here is something from the barrio, something black. Of blacks and made principally by blacks, which in a short time became something very much our own, related to our lives here in Cuba."

Earlier US black nationalists in the 1920s and the postrevolutionary period had not generated so much interest among Afro-Cuban people, who failed to strongly identify with their overt racial language. But among young Afro-Cubans who were increasingly feeling the effects of racial discrimination in post-Soviet Cuba, the black nationalist aspirations of US rappers were received with considerable enthusiasm. Black August also arranged for Cuban rappers to visit the US, where the Cuban group Obsesión opened for The Roots in New York, and important collaborations between Cuban and American rappers continue to this day.

In addition to these cultural relations that have expanded in the post-Soviet period, Afro-Cuban activists such as the writer Roberto Zurbano called for increased economic ties between Afro-Cubans and African Americans. He cited the relative advantages of white Cubans on the island as partly due to the established and wealthy white members of the Cuban diaspora in Miami and abroad who send remittances to their families in Cuba, a phenomenon that has accelerated the divisions between white and black Cubans.[3] Because Afro-Cubans don't have the same access to remittances as their white counterparts, Zurbano suggests that they could receive greater financial support for their small businesses and community-based organizations from black Americans. Since the establishment of diplomatic ties between the two countries and the entry of corporations such as Netflix, Zurbano has argued that for black Cubans to move out of poverty, they also need access to capital in order to start and sustain small businesses. Bringing in Netflix and Coca-Cola would not make opportunities available to people in the barrios, he argued. It must be done through the sharing of capital and resources in the black diaspora. While Afro-Cubans and African Americans have strong spiritual connections, he said, their political-economic relationships are not yet as strong as those between white Cubans on the island and in the diaspora.

Leaders and activists in both nations have called for greater strategic alliances that are built from the bottom up rather than the top down. Black Cubans can relate to the Black Lives Matter movement in the United States. Although the structures and histories of racial inequality are different in both countries, and black people in Cuba are not killed with impunity by police as they are in the United States, police harassment of black Cubans and racism more generally are pervasive. The heightened awareness of issues of racism in both the United States and Cuba represents an important opportunity for strengthening a dialogue between diasporic communities and finding new points of engagement.

Notes

This essay originally appeared in NACLA *Report on the Americas* 48, 1 (2016): 54–56.

1 Alejandro de la Fuente, *A Nation for All: Race, Inequality, and Politics in Twentieth Century Cuba* (Chapel Hill: University of North Carolina Press, 2001), 296.
2 Roberto Zurbano, "Soy un negro más: Zurbano *par lui-meme*," *Afro-Hispanic Review* 33, no. 1 (Spring 2014): 13–60.
3 Roberto Zurbano, talk to Encountering Cuba class, CUNY Graduate Center, November 17, 2015.

The Many Shades of Fidel Castro

On November 25, 2016, Cubans woke to the news that the ninety-year-old leader Fidel Castro had died. It was an event much expected and anticipated, given Fidel's ailing health and advanced years, but it still took Cubans and the world by surprise. It was a particularly hard blow coming so soon on the heels of the election of Donald Trump to the US presidency. In some ways these events represented the waning of one era, which was marked by wealth redistribution downward, international solidarity with oppressed peoples, and governance that favored the poor, to another signaled by the intensification of free-market capitalism, upward wealth redistribution, and a rhetoric about borders and walls that unleashes rampant xenophobia and racism.

The American mainstream media and hard-liner Cubans in Miami have long presented the Cuban socialist system as entirely dependent on the iron-fist leadership of Fidel Castro, with his much-awaited death leading to celebrations in the streets and the downfall of the system.

Yet this view is wrong on several counts. Fidel managed a transition in leadership to his brother Raúl in 2006, when his health started to decline. In practical terms, Fidel's death presented little to no challenge to the everyday functioning of the Cuban government. And when Raúl retired, there would be a transition in leadership to Vice President Miguel Díaz-Canel, ensuring continuity with the Castro brothers' policies and programs.

While there were mixed reactions in Cuba to Fidel's death, there were no large celebrations on the streets. This was only partly due to fear of reprisal: for many Cubans, particularly of an older generation, Fidel still represented the idealism and hopes of an earlier generation that they could create an independent and equitable socialist system on an island under the yoke of the United States. For all of Fidel's errors and flaws in leadership, and they were many, he pursued this dream single-mindedly for many decades. He survived numerous assassination attempts, outlived many US presidents, and always sought to extend the outreach of the Cuban Revolution abroad through solidarity with liberation struggles and medical and educational assistance, which will be some of his greatest legacies as leader of Cuba.

There was no quick transition to a market society as a result of Fidel's death. While the media has often presented Cubans as clamoring for market freedoms denied to them, the past few decades of experimentation with market reforms have resulted in widely increasing racial and economic divisions in Cuban society. Although the Cuban socialist system became dysfunctional after the collapse of the Soviet Union, the Cuban leadership has had to tread carefully in their market reforms to preserve the most important and cherished aspects of Cuban socialism, including the health care and education systems. Cubans could see the vast inequalities that opened up in Russia and Eastern Europe after the collapse of communism, and that was not a model they wanted to emulate.

Fidel was beloved by many for his charismatic style of leadership that kept him close to the people and to their concerns. A Cuban friend of mine, now in her mid-forties, recalled the day that Fidel came to her elementary school. There was no formal visit announced, and the children didn't even realize he was coming until they saw him enter the schoolyard with a few of his guards. He sat with the children and asked them about their day and what they were learning about in school. For my friend, that visit forever marked her view of the president as someone who cared about the people and wanted to hear their opinions.

At other times, he could be seen as a micromanager who demanded people's attention and allegiance. On the evening of September 11, 2001, Fidel reflected on the events of that day in a nationally broadcast address from a new elementary school that he was inaugurating. In front of a group of ten- and eleven-year-olds, Fidel expressed sympathy for the American people, offered the resources of the country for treatment of the victims, and urged caution on the part of the American government. In the middle of a statement about why the United States should not be carried away in a fit of rage and start dropping bombs on innocent people, he paused to reprimand a schoolgirl sitting at her desk: "Put down that pencil. Don't doodle. Try to pay attention while I'm talking."

Cuban musicians and artists tended to refrain from references to Fidel in their artistic productions, partly to avoid censorship. They sometimes used veiled references to Fidel, such as in Daniel Díaz Torres's 1991 film *Alicia en el pueblo de las Maravillas* (Alice in Wondertown). *Alicia* is a satirical comedy about a drama coach who goes to a small town called Maravillas for her obligatory year of community service. The director for the corrupt and mismanaged Sanatorium for Active Therapy and Neurology (SATAN) in Maravillas was rumored to be a caricature of Fidel, and the film was withdrawn from theaters after four days. In 1989, an exhibition at the Castillo de la Real Fuerza was closed when it was found to include a portrait of Fidel Castro in drag with large breasts and leading a political rally. This period was one of provocative political art and confrontations with the art establishment, but in the wake of censorship, artists again moved to safer topics.

Despite the intolerance of antiestablishment art in Cuba, Fidel showed himself willing to engage with new cultural genres, such as rap music during the 1990s. At a national championship baseball game in 1999, when the Cuban national team played the Baltimore Orioles, instead of the obligatory salsa song, the first pitch was preceded by a song from the Cuban rap group Doble Filo. The whole stadium rapped along, including Fidel Castro himself. American actor Danny Hoch, who was present at the game, called Fidel "the first world leader to embrace hip hop."

Maligned as "Castro the dictator" by some and loved by many others who referred to him endearingly as "Fidel," he was remarkable for his very survival in a world that sought to eliminate young black, indigenous, and Third World revolutionaries. Lumumba, Che, Sukarno, Malcolm, Allende, Anna Mae Aquash, Fred Hampton—all were gunned down before they could bring to fruition the visions of equality and justice to which they dedicated their lives. By sheer luck or ingenuity, Fidel and the Cuban Revolution survived to provide an alternative model of a socialist society. In the dystopian Trump era, it is important to keep alive the memory of what Fidel Castro and others of his generation stood for.

Note

An earlier version of this essay appeared in NACLA *Report on the Americas*, November 27, 2016.

PART III

CUBAN FUTURES AND THE TRUMP ERA

In this final section, the essays cover a moment of renewed hostilities from the United States under a Trump administration. Despite the hardships that Cubans suffered due to reimposed travel and trade restrictions, the vibrant cultural and social life of the streets of Havana and even the small towns of the rural provinces reflects a culture of resistance as Cubans continue to invent and hustle. Alternative social justice projects, such as a hairdressers' collective for social change and a children's documentary making group, fund themselves through proceeds from the tourist industry and sometimes spring out of long-standing grassroots collaborations with organizations outside the country. Cubans show a remarkable ability to continually invent and reinvent, especially under difficult circumstances. But what stands out time and again is the distinctly Cuban vision behind these projects, based in human solidarity and a collective spirit.

The Cold War Politics of Donald Trump

In 2015, Barack Obama declared a détente with Cuba, initiating, with Cuban President Raúl Castro, a normalization of relations between the two countries. But since his election in November 2016, Donald Trump has attempted to revert to an obsolete and aggressive Cold War policy by strengthening the economic embargo and promoting regime change. Trump's ill-conceived measures and bombast cannot undo all of the advances in US-Cuba relations that were made under the previous administration. But they have added to the insecurity and daily struggles of Cubans in a time of economic difficulty and the resurgence of the Right in the region. Those difficulties were compounded as the Cuban government addressed the lingering effects of Hurricane Irma.

Following his earlier threats to cancel the agreements between Cuba and the United States made under Obama, in November 2017 President Trump announced a set of new regulations to prohibit people-to-people travel, or individual visits by US citizens not with a tour group. The regulations also prohibited transactions with certain hotels and tour agencies that benefit Cuba's military and intelligence sector and expanded the list of Cubans who cannot receive funds from, or travel to, the United States. The regulations intensified a regime-change approach that seeks to destabilize the Cuban government rather than build links. They encouraged US travelers to patronize private businesses and to support dissident activities, while banning them from spending money on government hotels and resorts. Such an approach creates hardships for all Cubans—those who work in government-owned enterprises, those who supply them, and even those private businesses and private-home rentals affected by a decline in tourism resulting from the prohibition on individual travel.

Ordinary Cubans foresee dark times ahead. Those who have built up vibrant businesses or have been able to support their families through work in tourist industries are concerned about the downturn in tourism and their access to the coveted convertible peso (CUC). Others, mostly concentrated in the poorer barrios of the cities and rural areas, as well as the older population cut off from the tourist economy, still receive their income in the lower-valued Cuban peso and expect their own standard of living to decline further.

Shortages and blackouts are a part of everyday experience in Cuba, but in recent times it seems that everyone is trying to *resolver*, or resolve, a personal situation or crisis. One friend needs Benadryl for her son's allergies, but it is no longer available at local pharmacies for one peso (three cents) a packet, so she is forced to buy it on the black market, where a packet costs ten pesos (thirty-seven cents). Another suffers inflammation in her knees and has to wait until friends visiting from abroad can bring her supplies of Chondritin. Cubans go from store to store looking for basic necessities such as toilet paper. If they are lucky, someone may swipe packets of butter from a hotel so they can have it with their morning toast; butter is a delicacy rarely found in the local supermarkets. After Hurricane Irma struck Cuba's northern coast in early September, private construction suffered delays and setbacks, as many building supplies were diverted to helping victims of the hurricane and reconstruction efforts. The US measures only added to these difficulties.

For those Cubans who had to travel to the United States, either for work or to visit family, securing a visa became a real challenge. In October 2017, the US Embassy in Havana reduced personnel by 60 percent and stopped issuing visas to Cubans. The personnel were removed after the Trump administration alleged that sonic attacks had been carried out against members of the embassy. Soon after, the US State Department issued a travel advisory, warning about the possibility of such attacks in tourist hotels. In order to procure a visa, Cubans had to travel to a third country and apply for one there—an expense that most cannot afford. Members of the rap group Obsesión, for example, who had been planning a US tour, had to go to Colombia to apply for visas.

But despite all of these difficulties, there is still vibrancy in the cities and rural towns of the island. Cubans make do with what they have. Up and down the major thoroughfares of Havana, such as Calle Veintitres or Infanta, Cubans execute an intricate repertoire of gestures to flag down the shared taxis that

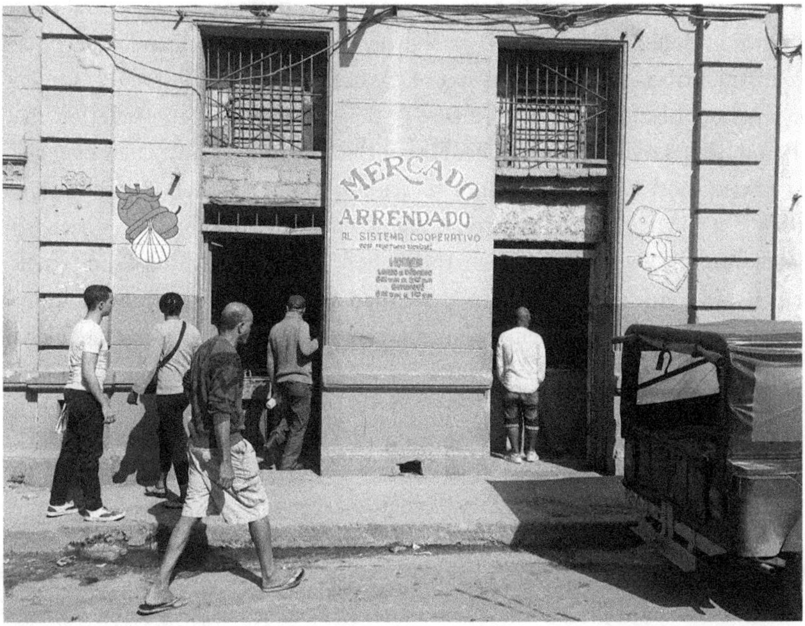

Figure 19.1 Cooperative Market. Photo by the author.

charge ten pesos per sector. A thumb pointing in a fixed direction indicates to the driver where the passenger wishes to go. Holding up three fingers to an empty cab indicates that the person wants a private ride to a nearby location and is willing to pay three CUC ($3.50) for the ride.

As Cubans queue up in long lines for the ubiquitous internet cards that provide up to five hours of web access in local hot spots for five CUC ($5.80), they are remarkably patient and gracious toward one another. As in all places where Cubans wait for services and transport, an arriving person will ask who is *el ultimo* (the last) and then wait behind that individual. If someone needs to push to the head of the line because of an emergency, there is no protest from the others in line, who just assume they must have a good reason to do so.

The cultural life of Havana is as upbeat as ever. At an art opening displaying the work of three black artists in the beautifully renovated space in Old Havana known as Factoria Habana, enraptured crowds populated the three floors of the gallery and poured out into the surrounding streets. In a week of cultural activities organized by Cartelera Cultural Cubana, there were free and inexpensive concerts by well-known Cuban artists such as the *trovador* Gerardo Alfonso and the black rock group Síntesis, as well as Colombian and Russian film screenings. Jazz musician Roberto Fonseca inaugurated a new cultural space known as Bule-Bar 66. There is no shortage of enriching cultural experiences to distract from or make poetry out of the hardships.

All of this amounts to a culture of resistance against the isolation that Trump wants to impose on Cuba. Rather than turning against their own government, most Cubans are angry at Trump, whom they see as taking them back to a failed and anachronistic Cold War politics. Cuba has never been isolated from the world, or even from the United States—something Trump's policies fail to comprehend. And now more than ever, people-to-people exchanges, travel, and contact will help Cuba to survive this period, as we create global solidarities to resist Trump's attacks.

Note

This essay originally appeared at TheNation.com, November 16, 2017.

Hairdressers of the World, Unite!

(You Have Nothing to Lose but Your Locks . . . and a Community to Win)

December 27 is celebrated in Cuba as the Day of the Barber and Hairdresser. The initiative was inaugurated by the prerevolutionary Cuban government in 1946, in honor of the barber, poet, and historian Juan Evangelista Valdés Veitía. In recent times, a local community project in the historic district of Old Havana known as Artecorte has sought to revive this holiday—and dignify the trade of hairdressing—with acts of public theater, hairstyle shows, and art festivals.

Beginning in 2010, Artecorte, together with the City Historian's Office, renovated a small stretch of Calle Aguiar, baptizing it "Hairdressers' Alley." They restored the facades of the old colonial-style buildings and repaved the sidewalks of the languishing street. At the entrance to Hairdressers' Alley there is a sculpture of a gigantic pair of scissors made of black steel by artist Alberto Matamoros. The inscription beneath it reads, "A Tribute to the Barbers and Hairdressers of the World."

The project has been driven by local resident and legendary hairdresser Gilberto Valladares Reina (Papito), who sees hairdressing as an art and hairdressers as central to organizing communities and bringing about change in their societies. Papito hopes to connect with barbers and hairdressers around the world by requesting that they send a pair of their old hairdressing scissors to Artecorte to be attached to the scissors monument along with the donors' names.

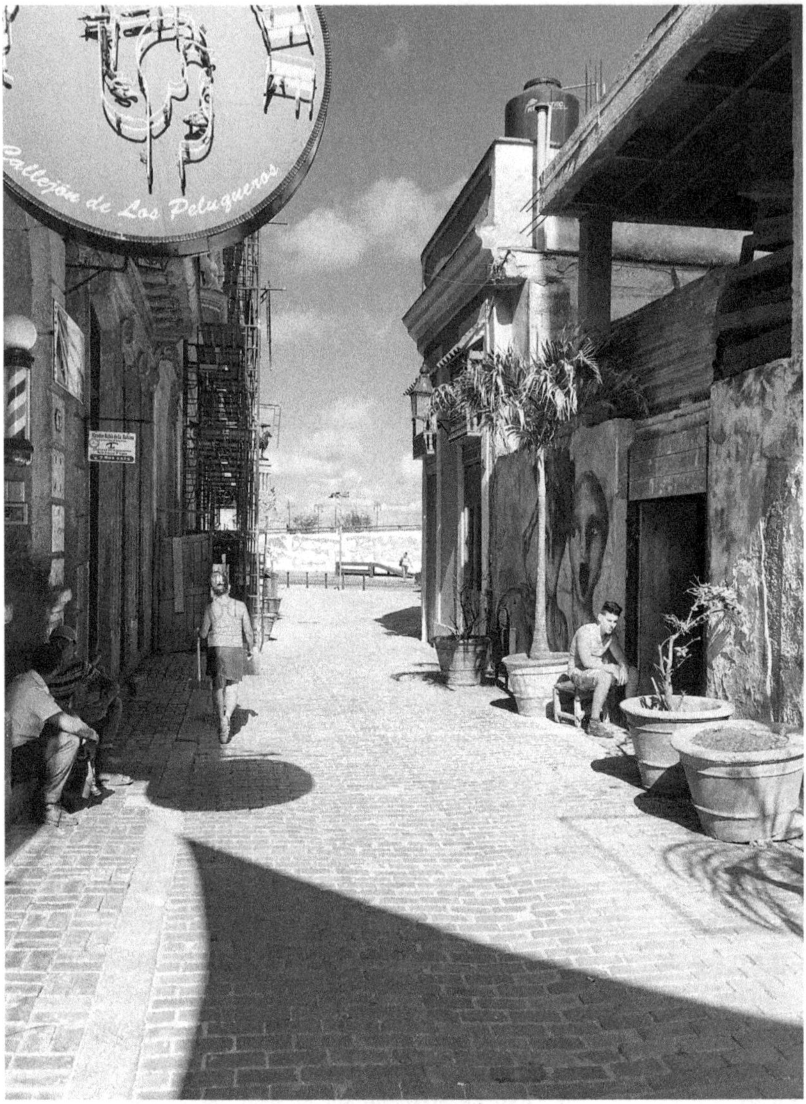

Figure 20.1 Hairdressers' Alley. Photo by the author.

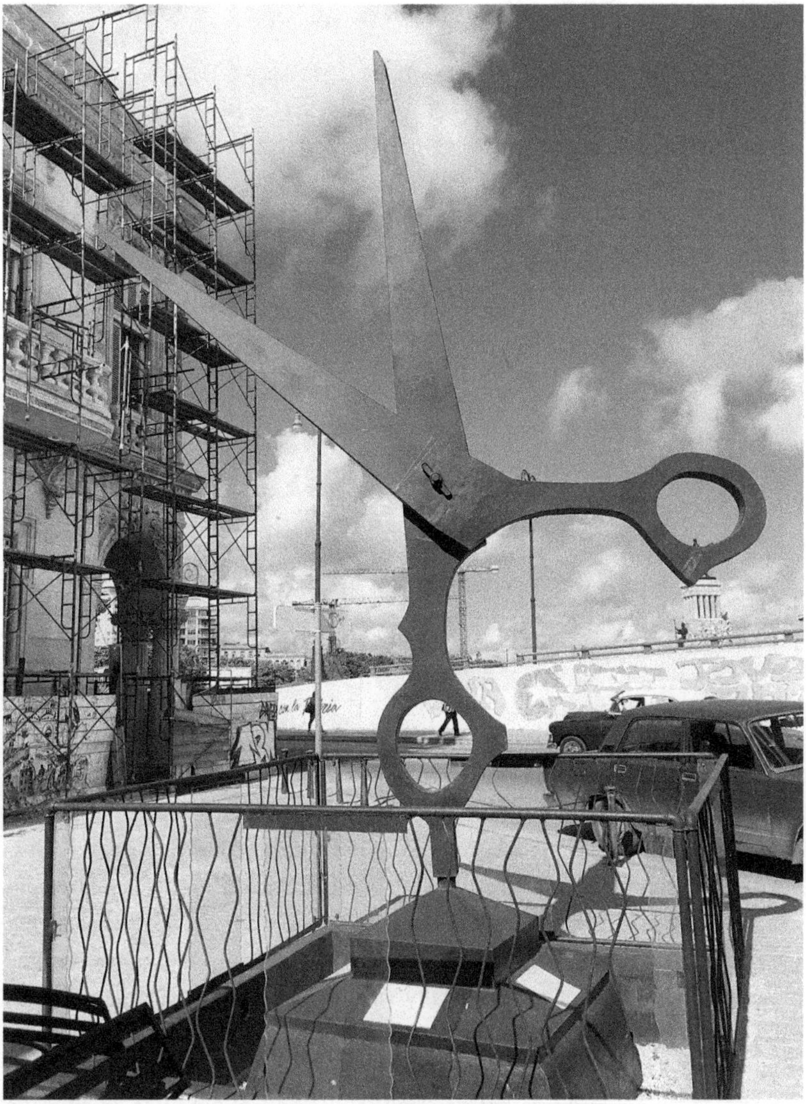

Figure 20.2 Sculpture of a pair of scissors by Alberto Matamoros. Photo by the author.

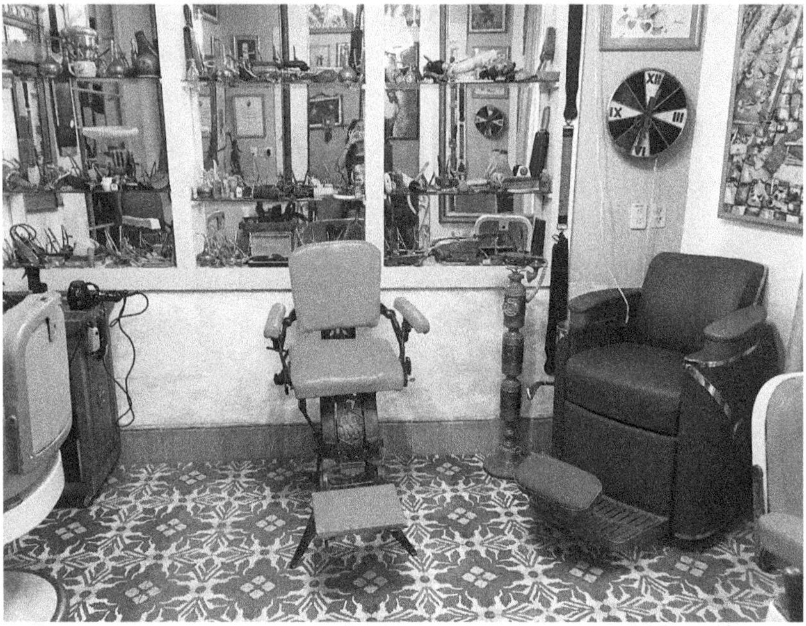

Figure 20.3 Papito's hair salon. Photo by the author.

Papito's hair salon, which also functions as a barbershop museum, is on the second floor of a walk-up building at the start of the street. It is filled with original paintings on the theme of hairdressing and antique collectors' items such as old cash registers, barber chairs, shaving brushes, and hairdressing equipment from the past century. A decade ago, this salon was the only business on what was a very poor street. Today, in this small stretch of only about one hundred meters, there are twenty-three locally run small businesses such as outdoor cafés and restaurants that employ more than one hundred people. The proceeds from these businesses are put back into the community, which includes a free bartending school and free hairdressing school on Calle Aguiar, in addition to a range of other activities in the broader Santo Ángel barrio. The walls and streets are filled with paintings, sculptures, and murals, as well as history placards showing old pictures of the street and the neighborhood from the nineteenth century.

Papito started the community school of hairdressing in 2010 to teach a trade to local kids, but now young people come from across the city to take his classes. The school is on the second floor of one of the colonial buildings that line the street. Papito, a light-skinned Cuban with a shaved head in his

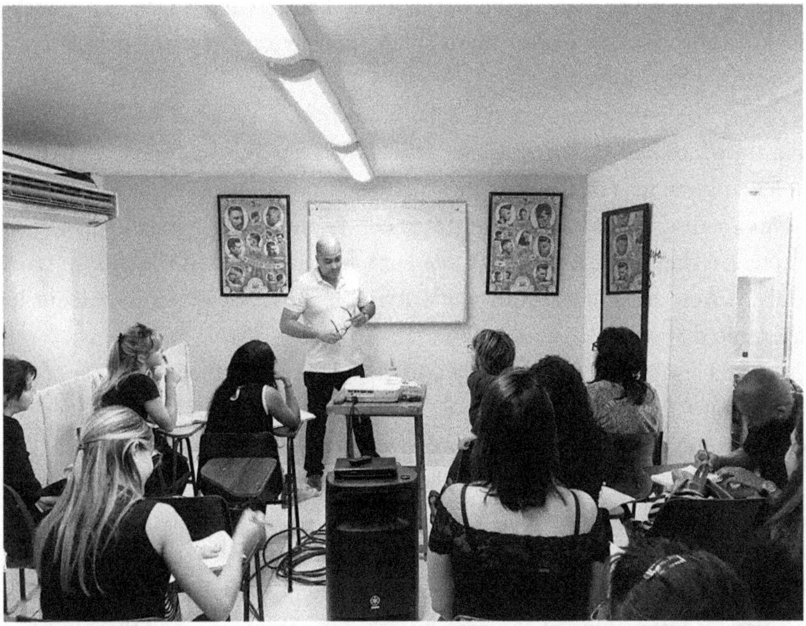

Figure 20.4 Community school of hairdressing. Photo by the author.

late forties, stands before a group of some twenty students all attired in black. He makes notes on a whiteboard, cleaning it with a cloth and some shampoo, as he philosophizes, entertains, and imparts history while bantering with the students, who seem to hang on his every word.

Part of the course involves learning the basic skills of the trade, but Papito wants to equip his students with much more than technical training. He emphasizes that hairdressing is not just about cutting people's hair. "We are artists, we are creators, we inspire," he tells the students, encouraging them to look for inspiration in films, videos, magazines, television, and even people walking by in the street. "One of the best fonts of inspiration is found in nature," he says. "Shape, color, and the rhythms and movement of waves in the sea have inspired painters, poets, composers, and stylists."

History is also fodder for inspiration. Pointing to the posters behind him—signature haircuts and barbershop classics from the 1940s—Papito tells his students to research hairstyles from earlier epochs with an eye to reinventing them. He says inspiration also frequently comes from street styles and nightspots. Papito wants to communicate to the students that the stylist is an artist who engages with society and works for social change. He says that this is not true in other parts of the world, where hairdressing is seen as a money-making business. “In Cuba,” says Papito, “hairdressers have the power to do something good for society.”

The students attending the school are from a range of backgrounds—mostly white and mixed race, but few black Cubans. One wonders if there is much awareness of the ways in which black hairstyles have long been seen as an art form and as a political statement. In the 1940s, African Americans expressed their identity through the conk hairstyle, and in the 1960s, Afro-Cubans wore natural Afros in solidarity with the Black Power movement in the United States.

Just a few houses up from the hairdressing school, in the upper floor of the Bar Cabaña, is a bartending school , where a visiting American bartender addresses a roomful of young Cubans dressed in red T-shirts with the logo of the French-Cuban company Havana Club, which funds the classes. He offers anecdotes and cultural explanations about such things as the home cocktail bar often found in American living rooms. Over a nine-month period, the students are trained in bartending skills; upon graduating, they will get a job in Cuba’s tourism industry. One of the prerequisites for acceptance into the course is English-language skills. The students are also taught about the history of cocktails in Cuba, so that they can entertain patrons with the information.

Both the bartending and hairdressing schools are affiliated with the Artecorte project, and the students are encouraged to volunteer in community programs in the Santo Ángel barrio. The students organize activities such as painting, sports, and clown shows for neighborhood children, and they facilitate a weekly dance party with a live DJ for older Cubans at the Nueva Vida senior center, one street over. They also collect donations of clothes, soap, and shampoo for the seniors and cut their hair.

When we arrive at the dance party, a ninety-year-old woman with her white hair tied in two buns has the microphone and is belting out the lyrics to “Que manera de quererte,” by the Puerto Rican salsero Gilberto Santa Rosa. She dances in step to the music coming from the DJ and sings with great emotion: “Where can I get wet if not in your laughter? Where can I drink you if not in your mouth?” An elderly man in a tank top and cap swivels his hips next to her, and a black woman in a red head scarf spins around and waves her arms in the air. A few others get up, shaking their hips as they dance with some of the students. The seated seniors whoop loudly, clap, and dance in their seats. “In what way can I love you?” they all chime in on the chorus. “In what way?”

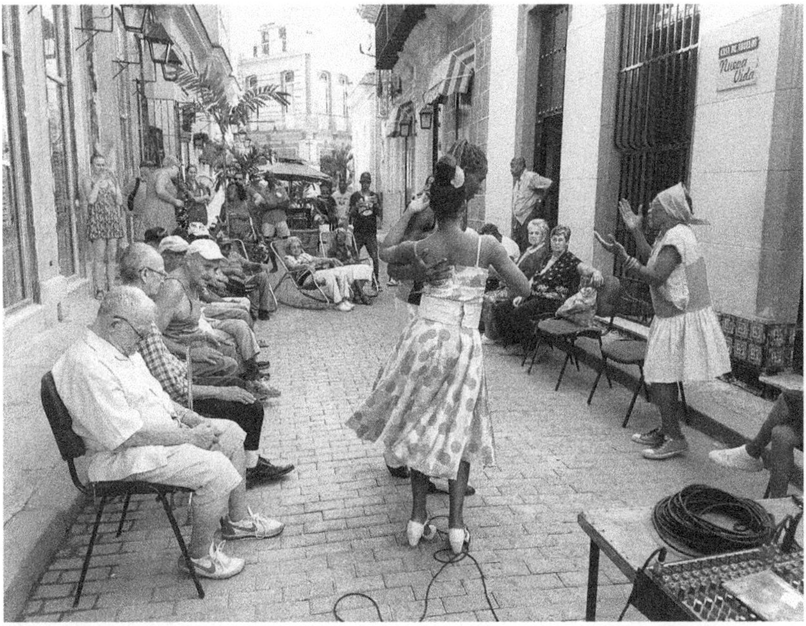

Figure 20.5 Dance party at the Nueva Vida senior center. Photo by the author.

Papito was born in 1969 in Santo Ángel. At the age of eighteen, he started working as a hairdresser in one of the state-run salons in the working-class neighborhood of Jesús María. Until 1993, when private businesses were legalized, almost all hairdressers and barbers were government employees. Papito opened his own private salon in 1999, where he has been working ever since. In the same year, he founded Artecorte.

The Cuban government authorized self-employment partly in response to the high unemployment that beset Cuba after the collapse of the Soviet Union. Licenses were permitted for a range of trades, and in 1995 small family restaurants, known as *paladares,* were legalized. By 1996, there were more than 200,000 small businesses in Cuba, and with additional reforms introduced by Raúl Castro in 2010, that number has reached about 535,000.

Overall, the government's approach toward small businesses has been incoherent. It has recognized the contributions made by these businesses to the national economy and in alleviating poverty in the face of reduced state services, but the government is also concerned about this sector's political role, which it fears may eventually pose a threat. At times, the government has withdrawn licenses in certain trades and reintroduced restrictive legislation. Small businesses are vulnerable to crackdowns and have often found themselves attacked by the media.

For some North American observers, the Cuban small-business sector represents the repressed spirit of entrepreneurialism that will liberate Cubans from the shackles of a state-managed economy. When then-US President Barack Obama visited Cuba in March 2016, he met with a group of Cuban entrepreneurs, including Papito. According to Papito, Obama told the assembled group that entrepreneurial youth in the United States face no limitations and can make $100 million just by working out of their garage. Papito, however, believed that such a system would not work in Cuba, where there is less of an individual drive to become a millionaire when so many cannot make ends meet, as well as a strong sense of solidarity with friends and neighbors who help one another out. "Culturally, we are different from the US and other parts of the world where everything is based in consumerism and individualism," he said. "Cubans are socialized differently."

Rather than joining a political opposition, many small-business owners such as Papito have become informal leaders of their communities. Popular Power is the official system of local representation that was put in place after the revolution to reflect the concerns of the local barrios at the municipal and provincial levels. Papito's father was a Popular Power delegate of the Santo Ángel barrio, and on one of the doors of Hairdressers' Alley, a notice announces an upcoming assembly for the nomination of Popular Power delegates. But in recent times, people have come to have less faith in this system due to the lack of government resources, resulting in the rise of informal leaders such as Papito, who can address local infrastructure problems with his own funds or by soliciting donations from local residents and businesses. "By being an informal leader, I can do a lot more," Papito says. "Things are not so politicized."

Papito has started a national network of hairdressers that has 150 members in smaller towns and provinces across the country. Part of his mission has always been to share knowledge of the trade with people outside Havana. One video shows a younger Papito with short, bleached-blond hair visiting some members of the network in the central provincial town of Santa Clara. A woman explains her attraction to the profession. "You have many dreams inside you, and this gives you a way to express them," she says. On December 27, 2007, three hundred hairdressers from across the country occupied the Plaza Vieja in Old Havana to mark the Day of the Barber and Hairdresser. This *corte simultáneo*, or "simultaneous haircut," was an act of theater that showed hairdressers rescuing the artistic values of the trade.

The Artecorte project has parallels with other urban-revitalization efforts in former industrial or working-class neighborhoods around the world. As with these other projects, there are concerns here that the regeneration is contributing to a gentrification that could eventually force out the original residents, who are most vulnerable. Indeed, the presence of groups such as Havana Club may signal moves toward shaping revitalization in the interests of the tourism industry and corporations. Yet unlike these other cases, Artecorte is directed by local residents, with barrio solidarity as their primary goal. "There is a crisis of values in our world today," says Papito. "We cannot solve poverty only with money. We also need a sense of commonality."

Note

This essay originally appeared at TheNation.com, December 28, 2017.

How Socially Engaged Activism Is Transforming Cuba

Since 1944, the rhythms of daily life in the small rural town of La Conchita in Cuba's western province of Pinar del Río have been tied to a bell that chimes at 7:50 a.m., noon, 12:50 p.m., and 5:00 p.m. This is the bell of the food-processing factory La Conchita, which has chimed regularly for over seventy years to alert the workers and their families to starting and closing times and the lunch break. The factory, which preserves and cans guava paste, pineapple chunks, bonito fish, tomato puree, and local produce, employs twenty percent of the town's population. Local residents work as machine operators, assembly-line workers, food technologists, and mechanics, jobs that span a range of skills and qualifications.

The factory was the lifeblood of the community, but it was making the workers and their families sick. The Soviet-era machinery and obsolete technology produced excess waste that clogged the nearby river with black sludge. The chimneys emitted thick plumes of smoke that caused respiratory problems such as asthma for residents and workers. There were high rates of cancer among community residents, particularly elderly people and children. In 2015, Cuban national environmental authorities announced the temporary closure of the factory. The announcement was devastating to a town that depended on the factory for its livelihood and existence.

In response to this decision, a group of local children between eight and fourteen years old made a documentary to record the history of the factory and show why it should be remodeled to reduce contamination rather than simply shut down. They named their film *Siete y 50* (Seven 50) after the factory's morning bell, which had served as a point of reference for the community. The girls and boys had received training in audiovisual production through a project known as Cámara Chica (Little Camera). Under the tutelage of Juan Carlos Baños Fernández, a producer at the local station Provincial TV, the children spent six months researching the history of the factory; interviewing their mothers, fathers, and grandparents who worked in it; and documenting the environmental impact. The project serves as an exemplar of socially engaged activism among a younger generation in Cuba who are finding new tools to tell their stories in a period of greater uncertainty and change.

The factory is an artifact of Cuban history and a symbol of the utopian vision of industrialism as progress. In the film, we see interviews with former directors, retired factory workers, and a local historian. La Conchita was inaugurated in 1944 by the two sons of the magnate Pío Ferro, one of whom later became a senator of the republic. During a new postwar era of mass consumption influenced by North American market culture, the factory turned Cuba's agricultural products into easily consumed commodities for middle-class households. After the revolution, the Ferro brothers left the country and on October 14, 1960, the factory was nationalized and expanded its export production. In the film, retired workers and former directors speak about the attempts to build worker-led management and a collective consciousness through popular assemblies and cultural activities. They recall Che Guevara's visit to the factory. A carnival in La Conchita brought a thousand people from the town together for a night of food and dancing.

The massive changes of that era are embodied in the director, a local black woman named Fara María Hernández. Hernández speaks about the challenges posed by the US embargo and the fall of the Soviet Union, such as the inability to replace obsolete machinery. In the documentary, she and other specialists discuss the solutions that could fix the problems: new technology that would minimize waste, a tall chimney to expel smoke far from human consumption, and testing of contaminant levels in order to reduce them. It's hard to question the importance of a factory that, as one worker says, is "the soul of the community," much less the underlying value of food processing in a system that has espoused consumer needs as part of the socialist ethic. As a result of the influence of the film, however, the factory was remodeled to reduce contamination and was allowed to stay open. For the children, it was clear evidence of the impact they could have through their storytelling.

On the highway leading to the town of La Conchita, tourist buses on their way to the popular holiday destination of Viñales tailgate slow-moving horse carriages. The streets of the rural town are unpaved and quiet, with most traffic consisting of pedestrians, bicycles, horse carriages, and the occasional motorbike or car. Over the past century, the population of the town has grown, as workers were drawn to the food-processing factory as well as a ceramics factory, which closed in 2017. The pastel-colored houses are small and rectangular, with flat roofs. One of them, on a small street off the main road, looks just like the others except for the artisanal woodwork on the front door and windows. This house belongs to Geovani Jiménez Izquierdo, known affectionately to the community as Pipo. Pipo has a successful business designing and selling artisanal wood furniture to large hotels and at trade fairs. He uses the proceeds of his business to fund a community cultural project in La Conchita known as Los Chapuserios, of which Cámara Chica is one element.

Pipo is an affable man in his mid-fifties with a shaved head and a shy smile. He came to La Conchita as a child from a rural area about five miles away known as Municipio Consolación. His parents were farmers, and his father was a musician in a local folkloric group. Pipo's father died when he was eleven, and his mother could not afford to raise all of her children, so she sent Pipo to live with his aunt and attend secondary school in La Conchita. After school, he stayed in the town. In 2006, Pipo began to design and build artisanal furniture: tables and chairs made of roughly hewn and polished slabs of wood, with no metal or screws. He started a small workshop in his backyard, gradually filling larger orders from hotels and businesses and expanding his clientele.

As Pipo's business grew and he started making more profits, he was aware that people in the small community of La Conchita viewed him with some suspicion. His neighbors in the town were mostly workers in the factories or vendors getting by from day to day, and they did not like the idea of someone so wealthy living among them. There was also a general discomfort with the growing wealth disparities in Cuban society, which had arisen after the legalization of small businesses, alongside other factors. The value of egalitarianism had been long ingrained by the revolution, and for years there was rough parity of salaries among all Cubans. Pipo himself felt a need to give back to the community where he had grown up, so in 2008 he founded the cultural project Los

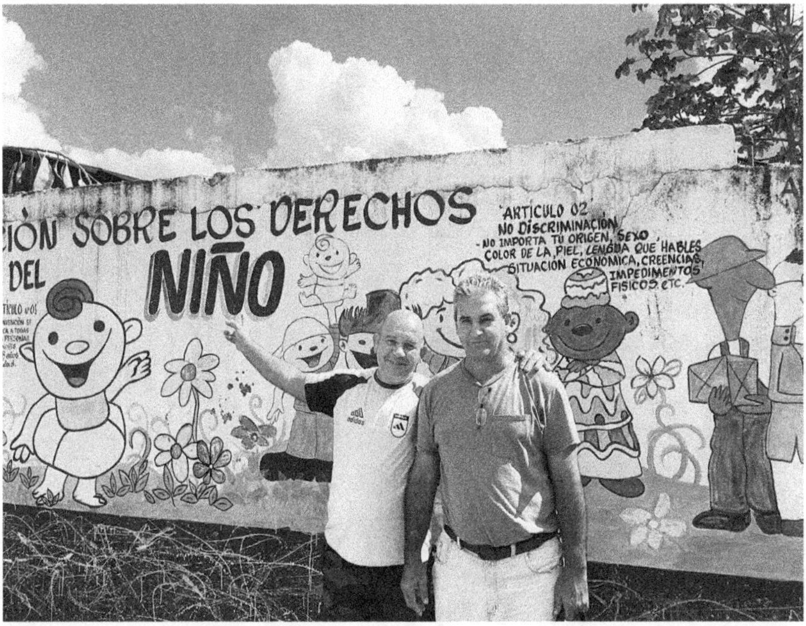

Figure 21.1 Geovani Jiménez Izquierdo and Juan Carlos Baños Fernández. Photo by the author.

Chapuserios, to provide a space for the town's children to engage in cultural activities such as dance, theater, painting, and music.

In 2016, the local ceramics factory, Fabrica Tejar, was slated to close, and Pipo saw an opportunity to expand both his growing business and the cultural project. He negotiated a deal with the Institute of Industrial Materials to renovate the factory space, renting part of it for his furniture workshop and giving the rest of it to Los Chapuserios to house a community cultural center, named Tejar Dolores. When he approached the people of the town with his idea, some were cautious, perhaps suspecting that he was trying to use them for his own ends. Others thought he would be providing a useful service and were interested in enrolling their children in a dance or music class. Pipo managed to convince them that he was handing over the space to them to renovate as a community-managed cultural space.

The first stage of renovations happened in February and March of 2017. Local people from the community volunteered their time to remove the rusting industrial machinery and clean the walls and rooms. Pipo built furniture

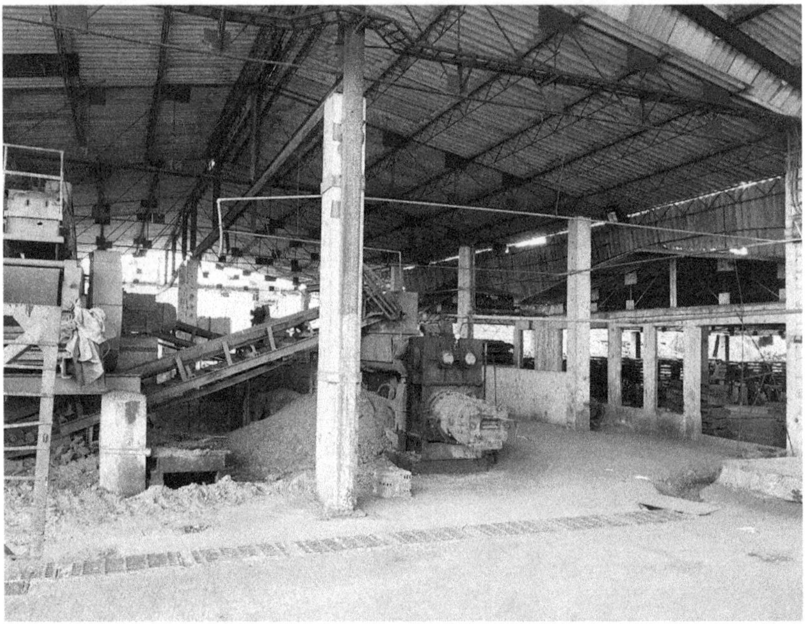

Figure 21.2 Fabrica Tejar. Photo by the author.

for the spaces and funded the construction of new bathrooms and other renovations. The cultural center consists of a library, with a full-time librarian paid by the government; a museum, with artifacts taken from the factory and the town; and rooms for art and theater classes and preschool activities. In the main courtyard is a stage for performances. Colorful murals illustrating the rights of children adorn the walls. Inside a tunnel, the paintings of the art teacher Luis Valdés and his students are displayed, and at the far end of the tunnel, some local women sell handicrafts on Sundays. On the other side of Tejar Dolores is the furniture workshop. Hundreds of wooden chairs, awaiting order and delivery, are used for meetings of Cámara Chica or other groups. There are piles of raw wood, cutting machinery, and workbenches.

For Pipo, running Tejar Dolores has been an elaborate balancing act that requires him to generate enthusiasm and participation from the community and assert the independence of the center, while also placating state cultural institutions. He has done everything according to the regulations: he negotiated with institutions to obtain the space, and he holds events such as a commemoration of the anniversary of Fidel Castro's death. But he doesn't want to turn it into a state-owned center or become beholden to cultural institutions that will oblige the children to perform at events when they are called and follow instructions from above. The funding from the furniture business allows the center a degree of independence that it otherwise might not have. For Pipo this is key. "The most important thing to emerge from this whole process," he said, "has been the involvement and participation of the community, in renovating the space, as volunteers, as students, donating time and resources."

The conversion of the Fabrica Tejar into a community cultural center mirrors the transformations taking place in Havana, where spaces such as La Fábrica de Arte Cubano (the Cuban Art Factory) were opened by the Cuban rock musician and artist X Alfonso in the renovated premises of a former cooking-oil factory in the suburb of Vedado. La Fábrica is anchored strongly in the visual arts, with several installations and exhibitions, but it also hosts cinema, music, and dance, promoting direct contact between artists and the community. By registering under the category of community projects, these centers are given official permission to occupy the unused grounds of state factories, but they are not as carefully monitored and regulated as private businesses. They are helping rejuvenate the postindustrial city and giving greater profile to the arts and cultural education, especially for a younger generation. This is even more valuable in rural areas such as Pinar del Río, that are often cut off from the cultural life of the cities.

On a Saturday afternoon in Tejar Dolores, the drama teacher Lizbeth Días, a young black woman with purple hair, is running through a rehearsal with a group of small children for a dramatic performance of the 1937 poem "Tourist in a Solar," by Afro-Cuban poet Nicolás Guillén (a *solar* is a working-class tenement, occupied mostly by black Cubans). The poem comically depicts residents of a solar, who are living four to a room and are sick with tuberculosis, as living the high life. Días directs the children, calling out stage directions, prompting lines, urging a little one to hurry up.

"Better than a luxury hotel," says Días, clapping her hands and calling out the lines to a plump little girl dressed in purple shorts and a tank top who emerges, sashaying her hips: "Stay in this solar / Here you will find plenty / What you won't find out there." A taller girl, playing the role of a solar resident with tuberculosis, comes out coughing. Another girl comments, "She didn't look after her cold / The idiot passed the day without a bite to eat." But then comes the crux of the anti-imperialist poem: "What one Yanqui has spent on alcohol alone, would have cured Juana."

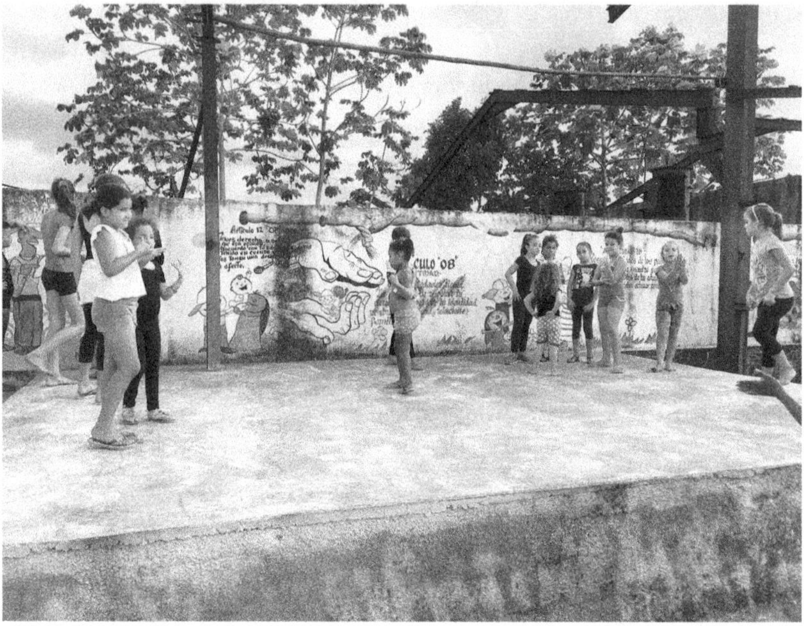

Figure 21.3 Drama rehearsal in Tejar Dolores. Photo by the author.

The community center is alive this afternoon. Art teacher Valdés and his students are organizing an exhibition of their newest works in the tunnel: landscapes of the mountainous Pinar del Río countryside, with glassy lakes, misty plains, and banana trees. Preschool children are engaged in group activities in the library.

Eight children from the Cámara Chica project, ranging from ten to sixteen years old, are meeting with TV producer Baños Fernández in the woodworking space. They look like tweens anywhere, playing on their cell phones (although none of them have internet access). Cámara Chica was launched in Cuba four years ago by the British Council, along with the Cuban education and culture ministries and the Arts Institute (ISA). It was implemented in six provinces across the country, including Havana. The idea was to bring audiovisual training and equipment to children who live in rural areas with less access to culture and film. In La Conchita, the Cámara Chica project began with a Handycam recorder, a MacBook for editing, and a microphone. The children were given the tools and training, but they decided on the stories they wanted to tell.

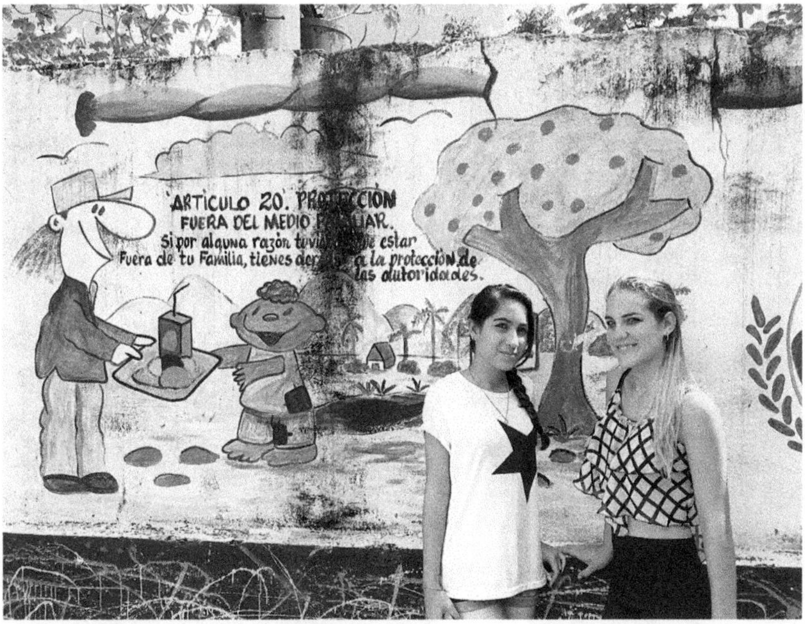

Figure 21.4 Alexandra Molina Morejón and Yusmila Alfonso Oliva, children from the Cámara Chica project. Photo by the author.

Many of the children were just eight or nine when they began with the project. Elisa Armenteros came from a mountainous zone in San Cristóbal, and when she moved to La Conchita she didn't know anyone in the community. Luis Rodriguez was bored and always getting into trouble. Both of them discovered an interest in filmmaking through Cámara Chica. On the television program *Convergencia*, they explain the process of the group: they meet together to come up with a theme and imagine how their ideas will look on the screen, then they plan their investigations, write the script, select the actors, and do the interviews. Alexandra Molina, fifteen, often appears as the anchor, confidently introducing subjects and doing spot interviews. On *Convergencia* she says, "Our methodology of work is to learn by doing."

The children have produced fictional pieces, public service announcements, short documentaries, and reports. Although overall direction is provided by Baños Fernández, the children carry out most aspects of production themselves, from writing scripts, acting, and interviewing subjects to filming, lighting, editing, and production. In addition to the film *Siete y 50*, they produced the documentary *Entre muñecas* (Among dolls), which tells the story of

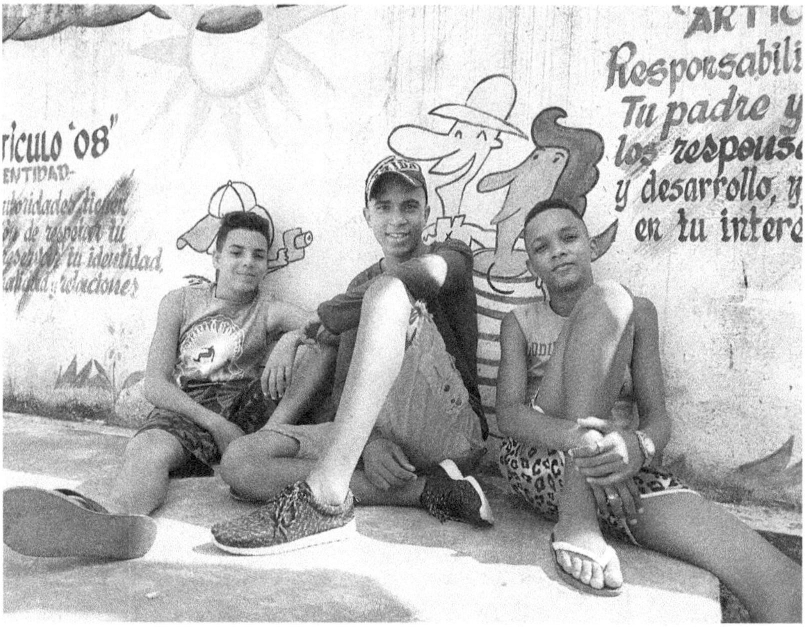

Figure 21.5 Frank Amed Pérez, Ray Michael García Torrens, and Alexander Hernández Mendoza, children from the Cámara Chica project. Photo by the author.

Sarita Vilaú, an older woman in the town who makes hundreds of dolls to keep her company and alleviate her loneliness. The public service announcements and documentary films have screened on local and national state television and at regional and international film festivals. The US-based nonprofit Americas Media Initiative (AMI) and its director, Alexandra Halkin, have been collaborating with Cámara Chica since 2014. In 2016, AMI facilitated a video-postcard exchange between Cámara Chica and the Baton Rouge ESL primary school LaBelle Aire. The films made by the children have been awarded over a dozen prizes. After a screening at the ISA in Havana, one girl was awestruck. “We got a standing ovation, as if we were great filmmakers!” she said.

The children have expressed interest in careers in filmmaking and audiovisual production. Sixteen-year-old Yusmila Alonso wants to study communications at the ISA, but residential scholarships are hard to come by. Alexandra Molina, who is passionate about filmmaking, would like to study cinema and be the TV host of a program for adolescents. Others feel that they don’t need a university education but can continue to train in the community and produce media where they live.

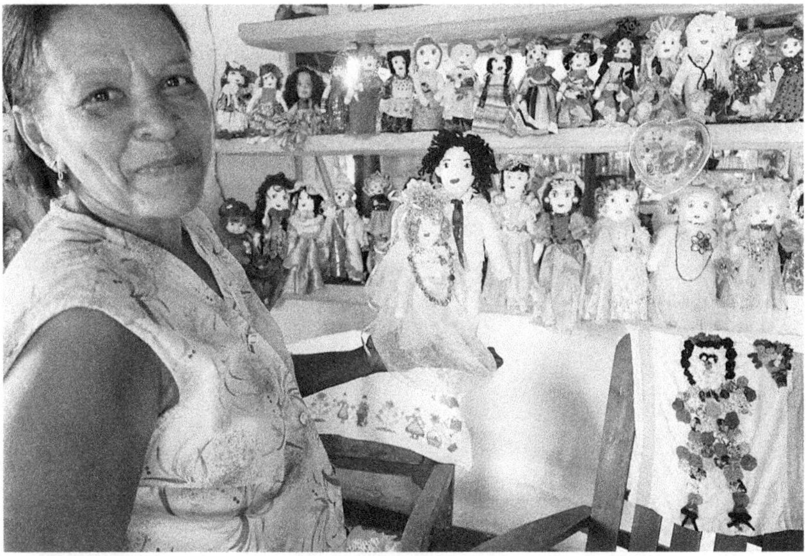

Figure 21.6 Sarita Vilaú with her dolls. Photo by Alexandra Halkin.

Coming from an outer province, the children don't often see their daily realities represented in the media. "We are the voice and the image of our community," Molina says. "We do what we do so that our community feels reflected in the media we create."

Note

This essay originally appeared at TheNation.com, February 22, 2018.

A Ship Adrift: Cuba after the Pink Tide

Cuba has been subject to renewed hostilities from the United States in the Trump era, but it also faces uncertainty given the decline of left-wing governments in the region and the ascendancy of far-right forces. Compared to the mid- to late 2000s, when Cuba benefited from a net of supportive allies across Latin America, chiefly Venezuela, recent years have seen the internal turmoil of leftist nations and the aggressive machinations of the Trump administration and its regional allies determined to break up the Cuba-Venezuela nexus.

In the early years of the post-Soviet period, when Cuba was reeling from the collapse of its main benefactor, a young Cuban emcee known as Randee Akosta rhymed, "We are a ship adrift that sails aimlessly, and without money, we've lost half our crew." He was referring to the economic and cultural isolation of Cuba in the 1990s. But with the demise of the regional left-wing allies who boosted the socialist nation during the boom of the Pink Tide, Akosta could have just as easily been rapping about the uncertain fate that Cuba is facing once again.

On March 4, 2019, the Trump administration announced that it would tighten the embargo against Cuba by authorizing lawsuits against Cuban companies that use properties confiscated after the 1959 revolution, under Title III of the Helms-Burton Act. Although the move applies to only about two hundred companies and appears largely symbolic, it presages larger measures, more sanctions, and travel restrictions against the island nation.

These moves can be read as retribution for Cuba's ongoing support of Venezuela as the Trump administration doubled down on its promotion of a regime-change strategy by means of a coup. The United States was one of the earliest and most enthusiastic supporters of opposition politician Juan Guaidó when he proclaimed himself president of Venezuela on January 23, 2019. Meanwhile, the administration's actions, such as meeting with defecting members of the military in Washington in 2018, indicated that it would back a military coup in the country. Sending humanitarian aid trucks to the Colombia-Venezuela border as a way to provoke conflict with the Venezuelan military also provided evidence of this confrontational strategy.

In addition to punishing Cuba, the tightening of the embargo is an attempt to put pressure on the island at a difficult time. Since Trump's early days in office, he has sought to strengthen the economic embargo and reverse the normalization efforts of the Obama administration. Trump also threatened to put Cuba back on the list of countries supporting terrorism, citing the influence of Cuban military advisers in Nicolás Maduro's government in Venezuela. Cuba was removed from this list in 2015 during the period of normalization.

Déjà Vu

Nearly three decades ago, Cuba faced a similar confluence of events. The Soviet Union collapsed, causing a massive economic crisis that famously led Fidel Castro to proclaim a special period on the island. Cold War triumphalism was in full effect, with free-market revolutions taking place in Eastern Europe in the midst of the global rise of neoliberal austerity policies. The Clinton administration also sought to push a beleaguered Cuba toward an Eastern European–style free-market transition by putting immense pressure on its economy and people through punitive policies such as the 1996 Helms-Burton bill.

Through a long and difficult process, Cuba pulled itself out of a severe economic recession by courting foreign investment from a range of countries, establishing joint ventures with foreign firms, developing its tourism sector, encouraging the flow of remittances, earning hard currency through providing overseas medical services, and taxing artists, athletes, and musicians working abroad.

Then, in the late 1990s, Cuba's fortunes turned around. Left-wing governments started coming into office across the region, in many cases powered by massive mobilizations of urban movements, peasants, unions, and indigenous peoples. A key ally for Cuba was the oil-rich nation of Venezuela, whose leader, Hugo Chávez, maintained close ties with Cuba's Castro. The rise of Chavismo helped bolster the Cuban nation, revitalizing it after the crisis of the special period. The Cuban economy received a boost through an agreement signed in 2000, which stipulated that Venezuela supply subsidized oil to Cuba in exchange for Cuba's sending health care workers, physicians, sports coaches, and arts workers to Venezuela, as well as offering free medical treatments to Venezuelans in Cuba. Venezuela also provided loans and grants to Cuba, planned to construct an underwater fiber-optic cable to improve Cuba's internet capacity, and agreed on a number of production and research projects on rice, nickel, and electricity.

The Cuba-Venezuela bloc also had symbolic importance as an alternative to US hegemony. Not just sailing aimlessly, Cuba was at the center of new regional initiatives such as the Bolivarian Alliance for the Peoples of Our America (ALBA), which sought to strengthen regional sovereignty in the face of ongoing attempts by the United States to impose its free-trade agenda. The Petrocaribe initiative launched by Chávez in 2005, which offered subsidized oil to debt-strapped Caribbean nations, displaced the political and economic power of US fossil fuel companies. As Bret Gustafson argues, the Petrocaribe initiative brought more energy sovereignty to the region, and although it was dependent on fossil fuels, it provided a vehicle for regional cooperation and a challenge to US oil hegemony over Caribbean nations.[1] Chávez, Castro, and Evo Morales of Bolivia were frequently photographed together, representing a new axis of hope for the socialist left.

The Rise of the Far Right

Chávez's death in 2013, along with the collapse of the commodity boom that had financed the Bolivarian Revolution, an opposition-led economic war, and economic mismanagement resulted in a growing crisis in Venezuela under Chávez's successor, Maduro. This internal crisis has had reverberations in Cuba, which was hit especially hard by decreased oil production in Venezuela. In 2019, Cuba received about fifty-five thousand barrels of crude oil per day from Venezuela, down from one hundred thousand barrels per day in 2014. With the rise of the Far Right, Cuba also has fewer allies in the region to count on for medical and other exchanges. In January 2019, eighty-three hundred Cuban doctors were set to withdraw from Brazil, after the newly elected far-right president Jair Bolsonaro questioned the terms of their contracts and qualifications.

For Cuba, there would be a significant impact if Venezuela were to succumb to a coup or right-wing takeover because it would mean the loss of a vital trading partner—albeit a weakened one—though it would likely not provoke a major crisis in the Cuban economy. In 2017, trade between the two nations totaled more than $2.2 billion, or 12 percent of Cuba's GDP. Still, Cuba's dependence on Venezuela is far less significant than its dependence on the Soviet Union in 1991. In recent years, the Cuban government has been looking for alternative oil sources, and in 2018 it signed a three-year agreement with Algeria to exchange crude oil for doctors. And the Cuban economy has some level of autonomy through the growth of diverse foreign investments, revenue received through tourism and remittances, and new trade agreements with US companies initiated under the period of normalization. Although the stricter travel regulations put in place by Trump reduced the number of American tourists in 2018, by the end of the year numbers had bounced back to 4.75 million international visitors, largely buoyed by a 48 percent increase in cruise ship arrivals and visits from Cubans residing abroad. These may mitigate the difficulties somewhat—and the revolution's chances of survival.

Cuba still has some left-wing allies in the region, especially following the election of Andrés Manuel López Obrador in Mexico, as well as in Uruguay and Bolivia. While these nations would be unlikely to replace the economic muscle of an alliance like Petrocaribe, they may provide some moral support for Cuba, as they have done to varying degrees for an embattled Venezuela.

What Next for the Left—And Cuba?

As far-right forces ascend in the region, what is the fate of the leftist and revolutionary governments that supported Cuba? As well as being under attack by long-standing imperialist and hegemonic powers, they have become victim to their own developmental logics and extractivist policies, which depend on highly fluctuating and ecologically finite resources such as oil. As in Venezuela, the massive infrastructural projects undertaken as part of the Citizens' Revolution in Ecuador under Rafael Correa were made possible by oil rents in the context of high oil prices, which collapsed by 2014. This was also the case in Bolivia's gas-fueled social revolution. The underlying economic model of "twenty-first-century socialism" needs rethinking, especially given the climate crisis currently threatening the planet.

These governments have also been marked by an unbalanced concentration of power in the figure of the presidency and a top-down approach to solving issues such as poverty. But although the Pink Tide as an electoral phenomenon dependent on highly charismatic leaders is in decline, the social forces that brought these leaders to power continue to struggle at the grassroots. From the Landless Workers' Movement in Brazil, to the communes in Venezuela and indigenous movements in Ecuador and Bolivia, social movements hold the key to an ecologically sustainable, democratic, anticapitalist future for the region.

For these grassroots movements and others, Cuba still stands as a symbolic pole, reminding us that human society can be organized on the basis of solidarity, cooperation, and respect. This is a profound vision that stands clearly at odds with the individualist, profit-driven mantras of far-right leaders such as Trump and Bolsonaro. Cuban society itself has been undergoing a much-needed transformation from within, as local neighborhood associations, cultural groups, and antiracist movements are challenging old dogmas and introducing new means of participation.

In a global era, Cuba will find a means of re-creating and fostering alliances. At a moment when "democratic socialism" has come back into the parlance of dominant presidential and parliamentary contenders, and people are looking for an alternative to failing systems of neoliberal capitalism, Cuba may well emerge once more as a buoy.

Notes

An earlier version of this essay appeared in NACLA *Report on the Americas*, April 1, 2019.

1 Bret Gustafson, "The New Energy Imperialism in the Caribbean," *North American Congress on Latin America* 49, 4 (2017): 421–28.

EPILOGUE

In the space of three decades, Cubans experienced the demise of their major Soviet benefactor. They witnessed successive US administrations that tightened the embargo, then reestablished diplomatic relations, and then pursued open regime change. They were buoyed during a renewed left turn in the region and then isolated as successive revolutionary projects in the region collapsed around them. Cuba has been tossed about on a sea of changing political fortunes, vulnerable to each policy shift from the North.

Remarkably, the island has survived the most difficult days: the massive economic crisis of the special period, the death of Fidel Castro, and, so far, the aggressive machinations of the Trump administration. In the process, the state has also adapted to new times by relaxing economic and political controls. But what has truly maintained the spirit of the Cuban people across these turbulent decades has been a culture of invention and everyday hustle. To speak of these in the Western individualist terms of entrepreneurialism is to misrepresent something far more rooted in histories of collective struggle.

The forms of cultural expression that emerged in the post-Soviet period have been marked by two features. One is their engagement and dialogue with global networks. The global culture industry has opened up new possibilities for addressing marginalized themes such as race and sexuality, while also introducing new market logics into the production of Cuban culture. Transnational NGOs and cultural movements such as feminist organizations and hip hop culture shaped emerging feminist and antiracist movements on the island. The second is their negotiation with state institutions, which has made available new channels for accessing power while delineating the boundaries of acceptable criticism. While drawing on resources from state and market, artists and activists have also used their platforms for a critique of new hierarchies of power in a globalizing Cuba.

Cubans have navigated the tricky labyrinths of the global market and the state to tell their stories in all of their richness, humor, and boldness. Coming out of the difficulties and contradictions of life in the special period in the late 1990s, artists took to public spaces and street corners to express themselves.

Art students curated a transvestite show in an art school and staged a performance in a shopping mall, rappers rhymed about the reality of life in marginal barrios, and an Afro-Cuban artist acted as a street vendor selling a black doll in the market.

The availability of digital technologies and social media in the new millennium gave cultural producers new vehicles for staging their concerns. Documentary filmmakers used small digital cameras and cell phones to tell stories of farmers struggling in the Sierra Maestra and collapsing buildings in Central Havana. With limited access to the global internet, Cubans made use of the state-run intranet to develop platforms such as SNet to connect local communities and the Cuban version of Wikipedia known as EcuRed. Through flash drives they circulated a range of material downloaded from the internet in a phenomenon known as the Weekly Packet. As with the hip hop movement's use of traditional instruments such as the Batá drums, because they lacked access to sampling technology, Cubans continued to turn deprivation into a source of innovation.

Cubans have created all kinds of spaces for expression, even in unusual and unexpected ways. Hairdressing has been used as a tool for self-expression, and an abandoned ceramics factory was remodeled to create a community cultural center in a small town. Unlike their counterparts in the West, Cuban teenagers do not have unlimited apps and games to distract them on their phones; one group made their own fictional pieces and documentaries about the stories of their communities.

What many of these cultural phenomena share is a broader concern with social justice. Even when propelled by global markets and NGOs, cultures take on their own local shape, oriented toward the community. This is the legacy of the ideals, educational systems, and shared ethos of the Cuban Revolution. The hairdressing school in the barrio of Santo Ángel involves its students in organizing activities for the children and seniors of the neighborhood. The young filmmakers of La Conchita made a documentary about the imminent closure of a factory that was the lifeblood of their community.

Cultural art forms have been closely connected with the development of social movements in Cuba, although unlike the covert programs designed by USAID to infiltrate Cuban hip hop and create a Cuban Twitter, they rarely had the aim of fomenting dissent and overthrowing the Cuban government. Afro-Cuban artists and hip hoppers used their art to raise issues of race and racism in Cuban society. They sowed the seeds for a rich array of racial justice organizations in the new millennium, such as ARAAC, the Red Barrial, and Alianza Unidad Racial. Artists have been at the forefront of social justice initiatives.

Organizations such as Color Cubano and Magín have been led by artists, poets, and writers. The musician Silvio Rodríguez embarked on a tour of marginalized barrios to share his music with residents and understand their everyday struggles.

It is not possible to predict how the future will unfold in Cuba, though the revolution faces better odds of survival at the end of the 2010s than in the early 1990s, despite the regional crisis of the Left. What we can say is that Cubans will continue to find ways to hustle, invent, create, and make poetry out of the material of their everyday life.

CPSIA information can be obtained
at www.ICGtesting.com
Printed in the USA
BVHW092042301220
596742BV00006B/954